"Italy's best is not just the material things that come from this great country, but the Italian lifestyle in general. Every single one of us will face life's challenges and personal losses, and I know of no one better suited than Dr. Raeleen D'Agostino Mautner for teaching how to incorporate the benefits and pleasures of the Italian lifestyle into our daily lives. Her own warm and heartfelt personal experiences and the knowledge she shares in this exceptional book will have you, too, enjoying the *limoncello* of life."

—**Richard J. Michelli,** founder and executive director of ItaliaLiving.com

"Dr. Mautner's poetic book not only helps shorten and heal grief, but also helps turn the healing into an opportunity to grow into a stronger, healthier, more vibrant, and more resilient person. The fresh intercultural perspective shows readers of any ethnicity how to move forward following hardship using the timeless Italian traditions of beauty, simplicity, and creativity. Self-renewal awaits those who turn the pages."

—**Martin Kantor, MD,** Harvard-trained psychiatrist and author of *Now That He's Out: The Challenges and Joys of Having a Gay Son*

"Dr. Mautner's writings convey a historical memory, without which man is like a tree without solid roots: weakly anchored to the ground. Her writing evokes and gives back a cultural belonging that unites us on earth in a holistic way. Only a forward-thinking mind like hers can combine aspects of the psyche with motions of the everyday aspects of life. In *Lemons into Limoncello*, she harmonizes all the components of the human personality, going deeper than just what is at the surface, never forgetting how much of life is due to poetry and art. One needs to have the strength of Atlas to support the entire world on their shoulders, to love everything, even the darkness, and then leave a beam of light. My dear cousin Rachelina (Raeleen) gives us this beam of light in a world of frequent suffering."

—**Giuseppe De Filippo,** internationally acclaimed artist and teacher in Calabria, Italy

"An uplifting book—written with an Italian passion for life—that provides excellent guidance for those suffering the loss of a loved one or other personal crisis."

—**Theodore Grippo,** attorney and author of *With Malice Aforethought*

"Through her own adversity, Raeleen Mautner has uncovered and presented to us a wonderful cultural philosophy that we all ~~~ ~~~~ hance our everyday life."

—**J. Ferrara,** supervising and Warren-Tricomi Sal

"For centuries Italians have weathered every tragedy imaginable—foreign occupation and oppression, famines, devastating illnesses that carried away babies as well as adults, poverty, injustice, and terrible wars waged by other nations and fought on their own lands.

"At the same time, Italians—both as a people and as individuals—have developed an enormous respect for life and an innate ability to appreciate even its smallest gifts: a sunny day; a cup of espresso; a family meal; or even a heartfelt love song. Adversity has taught them how to confront disasters and endure if not overcome them.

"In her excellent study, Raeleen Mautner, Ph.D. captures the remarkable gift Italians share with the world about how to live through the inevitable reversals of fortune that life brings with it . . . and still smile."

—**Dona De Sanctis**, editor-in-chief, *Italian America Magazine*

"Keenly conceptualized and elegantly articulated, *Lemons into Limoncello* provides the reader with a series of well thought-out suggestions on how to confront the aftermath of those life-changing traumas we all face. With the combined spirit of the Italian concept of *l'arte dell'arangiarsi* and the classical exhortation of *Spes ultima dea*, this book offers an Italian-style roadmap on how to move forward *pian piano* and, above all, *sorridere e mollare* as we so proceed. It should be required reading for all!"

—**Anthony Julian Tamburri**, dean, John D. Calandra Italian American Institute, Queens College/CUNY

"Perhaps life has knocked you down one too many times. Or maybe you've just gone 'stale.' Dr. Mautner is part philosopher, part psychologist, part life coach—but entirely Italian. She offers Italian-style therapy: food, family, friends, and fun—a recipe for your own, personal renaissance. What would Freud say if he was Italian? Here's your answer!"

—**Steve Perillo**, CEO, Perillo Tours

"Dr. Mautner has a real gift for translating the wisdom of our Italian cultural heritage into simple strategies for getting through life's challenges. An inspiring read!"

—**Paul Basile**, editor, *Fra Noi* (The Chicago-area Italian-American magazine)

"As a first-generation Italian American, it was an absolute delight to experience how this work melded our culture's approach to life with dealing with personal crisis. I highly recommend it to anyone for help during difficult times. A self-help book with a wonderful Italian flare!"

—**Andre' DiMino**, past national president, UNICO National

LEMONS
INTO
Limoncello

From Loss to Personal Renaissance with the Zest of Italy

Raeleen D'Agostino Mautner, PhD

Health Communications, Inc.
Deerfield Beach, Florida

www.hcibooks.com

This book is meant to be an educational work and in no way a substitute for professional help when needed. Neither the author nor the publisher is responsible for the outcome with respect to your choice to follow the ideas and strategies in this book. To maintain the privacy of the people and stories referred to throughout the book (other than the author's personal story), all names and identifiers have been changed or modified.

Library of Congress Cataloging-in-Publication Data

Mautner, Raeleen D'Agostino.
   Lemons into limoncello : from loss to personal renaissance with the zest of Italy / Raeleen D'Agostino Mautner, PhD.
        pages cm
   Includes bibliographical references and index.
   ISBN 978-0-7573-1734-7 (pbk.)
   ISBN 0-7573-1734-0 (pbk.)
   ISBN 978-0-7573-1735-4 (epub)
   ISBN (invalid) 0-7573-1735-9 (epub)
   1. Loss (Psychology)   2. National characteristics, Italian.   3. Social values—Italy.
I. Title.
   BF575.D35M346 2013
   155.9'3—dc23
                                                                                        2013004585

Publisher: Health Communications, Inc.
            3201 S.W. 15th Street
            Deerfield Beach, FL 33442-8190

Cover image ©JeniFoto, 2012. Used under license from Shutterstock.com
Cover and interior design by Lawna Patterson Oldfield

To Thomas Michael Mautner
(1951-2008)

Per Sempre

Quando soffri, quando senti dolore, quando ti senti deluso, quando ti senti confuso, quando ti senti tradito, quando ti senti perseguitato, quando ti senti usato, quando ti senti sfruttato, quando ti senti manipolato, quando ti senti deriso . . . entra nel profondo del tuo cuore. Lì vi troverai l'energia, la Luce per poter continuare il tuo viaggio.

When you suffer, when you feel sorrow, when you are disappointed, when you feel confused, when you feel betrayed, when you feel persecuted, when you feel used, when you feel taken advantage of, when you feel manipulated, when you feel put down . . . enter into the depths of your heart. There you will find the energy and the Light to be able to continue your journey.

—Dr. Valerio Albisetti, *Come Attraversare la Sofferenza*

Sommario
CONTENTS

Prefazione
FOREWORD

I am spending my usual period of spiritual retreat in rigorous solitude where I read, pray, and meditate in the silence of my stone hermitage. This treasure was built centuries ago on the top of a hill, surrounded by woods that are inhabited by deer, wild boar, and fox, in the Tuscan countryside in Italy.

I just finished reading this book you now hold in your hands. As I close the book, I breathe the scent of wildflowers from the pages where I still feel the lingering spirit of Raeleen Mautner's femininity, her sweet and strong soul. Thank you, Raeleen, because in reading your pages, I reconnect with my own feminine side, which I had for so long forgotten, and with my Italian side, which I had long ago relegated to a remote corner of my heart. Thank you for inducing whomever reads *Lemons into Limoncello* to breathe the air of the best that Italians represent and experience how the spirit of our people has enriched all of humanity.

The language Raeleen uses is rich with compassion and energy that heals the reader, without noticing the commitment such reading requires, as one relishes the joyful sensation of Italian living through the ancient and wise recipes that I would call the real and true food for the soul.

Slowly, Dear Readers, *Lemons into Limoncello* will carry you away to where you will no longer fear and no longer experience anguish. If you absorb its ideas, you will not remain brokenhearted, despite your life's difficulties. Your suffering will be transformed into a place where you learn new things, profound things that otherwise you might have never known.

Our ancestors, like those mentioned in this wonderful book, knew that sufferings show up to tell us something. They always hide a treasure. They give us useful directions for advancing on our journey of physical, psychological, and spiritual rebirth. They are bearers of change. They offer us the possibility to evolve and to grow. They offer us an opportunity.

The pages of *Lemons into Limoncello* bring about our true psychospiritual search, the kind that marks the very existence of each one of us. Raeleen uses her personal experience to help her readers, whom I call "travelers of the spirit," in an historic moment in which our contemporaries are facing a profound crisis of reason, of meaning. A loss of hope.

Lemons into Limoncello is for everyone, and above all, it is for those who don't confuse their spiritual journey with the roles they assume on earth. It is for those who don't wish to belong to groups that indoctrinate, or those who need to follow someone who purports to know everything. It teaches us never to despair and to believe that behind every loss, there is always meaning and hope. And that becomes evident from the great traditions of myth, symbols, and the kind of wisdom that renders it easier to recognize spirituality in everything and in every encounter.

For Raeleen, as for me, everything has meaning. There are no roads without exits, no lives that are useless, no mistaken encounters, no wastes of time. The universe in which we live is enchanted. Mysterious. With a story to tell. To live.

God does not live separately from men. If our journey is to be authentic, it means enabling us to understand how God speaks above all through failure, disgrace, violence, joy, encounters, sexuality, and the parts of us that lie in the shadows. It is a journey from the bottom to the top. Whether you are aware of it or not, the spirit that resides in the deepest part of each person's heart—no one excluded—is sacred and very powerful. *Lemons into Limoncello* is a book that will help you to reawaken that spirit and encourage you to live an even richer, more authentic life than ever before.

—**Valerio Albisetti**

Valerio Albisetti is considered one of the most distinguished presences in contemporary psychoanalysis. After having a successful psychotherapy practice and university professorship, Valerio Albisetti now dedicates his time to writing books on psychospirituality that have been distributed worldwide and translated into many languages.

Ringraziamenti
ACKNOWLEDGMENTS

THOMAS MICHAEL MAUTNER was the primary inspiration for this book. It is hard to find words to describe how grateful I feel for having had Tom in my life. While not of Italian heritage himself, through me Tom became an Italy enthusiast and believed strongly in my ability to translate my cultural heritage into self-help tenets that could really help people live happier lives. He was truly a great and loving man, with a deep sense of joy for the little things and a passion for the dimensions of life that Italians hold so dear, primarily *famiglia* (family).

Many thanks to Candace Johnson for her invaluable editorial perspective in shaping this book to be all it could be. Candace believed in this project from the start, and through her skill, intelligence, and support, she made it easy for me to do what writers love to do best.

I would also like to thank the staff at HCI for working so diligently on the details that make for a great book.

Mille grazie (thousand thanks) to Dr. Valerio Albisetti, whose book *Come Attraversare la Sofferenza* offers me insight and hope whenever I turn through its pages: I thank you for your genuine kindness and willingness to write the foreword to this book; most of all, for your ability to change lives through your inspiration each and every day.

With endless love and appreciation for Casey, Thomas, and Dennis—who bravely travel forward on their life's journey without the father who loved them so dearly. Dad would be so proud of all of you for the way you have evolved and incorporated in yourselves the best of his qualities. May all of your dreams be realized in this lifetime. Your faces, your smiles, and your thoughtfulness toward me are my daily reminders that your dad is still here and that his joy for life has had a lasting effect on us all.

Mille grazie (thousand thanks) to my cousin Giuseppe De Filippo, a true intellectual and artistic genius, who carefully double-checked my Italian words throughout this text.

Finally, to my father, Marino D'Agostino, and our family in Castelpagano—you are the exemplars of what it really means to live *la dolce vita* (the sweet life) despite the hardships.

Introduzione
INTRODUCTION

THE RENAISSANCE WAS A PERIOD of cultural rebirth on the literary, philosophical, and artistic fronts of ancient Greece and Rome. It was the dawn that brought the long dark "degenerate" (as painter Giorgio Vasari described it) Middle Ages to new and unimaginable heights of enlightenment, and even genius. On a broader yet much more personal scale, I think of the Renaissance as an exquisite metaphor for how even the darkest periods in our own lives are followed by a dawn that is brighter and more enlightened than the stretch of time that preceded it. It is not that tragedy itself leads to a better existence, but rather the insights born of our ability to cope, to go forward, and to live once again as if we are deserving of joy. Personal evolution is the real gift that becomes apparent in the wake of our crises.

All major transition comes with some degree of loss. When your life changes, for better or for worse, you lose the familiarity that once grounded you, and you feel like you've been thrust into the "twilight zone." You find yourself longing for a past (or parts of the past) that you can't get back, and panicking about your ability to handle the unknown

1

future. Getting married or having a baby are joyful examples of important life transitions, but even those changes can be hard, as they require you to lose some aspects of your "old life" that made you feel secure. Unhappy loss, however, is the focus of this book, because most of us have a much harder time dealing with this kind of adversity. When you lose a loved one, for example, you are losing a part of your own identity in addition to losing every role that person filled in your life. When you lose your home, you may also lose your self-esteem, the community that surrounded you, and the roots you built in your neighborhood. When you lose your job, you may lose your means of paying the bills, providing for yourself and your family, engaging in social activities that cost money, and even the ability to buy the clothing it takes to make yourself presentable enough to go to a job interview. When you lose your health, you may be forced to give up your goals and dreams, and you may also lose your ability to interact with the world around you in a vibrant way. Loss is such a regular part of life that it is foolish of us not to expect it. Yet we are thrown off by its impact almost every time.

Inherent in the traditional Italian culture is an unquestioning acceptance of both hardship and victory. Both aspects of the human condition comprise the threads that, when woven together, create the richness of life's fabric. Acceptance of reality, albeit painful, is the first step toward personal resilience and a new beginning where the pain associated with your loss becomes a distant memory. What I learned from my ancestors is that nothing about loss itself—no matter how traumatic—has the power to sentence us to a life of misery. In fact, the best antidote for loss is a win. You deserve to win back your passion for life. My hope is that the ancient and contemporary wisdom of Italy, its everyday traditions, and its time-tested philosophies will help you do just that.

Who This Book Is For

Lemons into Limoncello is for those who have recently (or not so recently) faced a major personal crisis. It is for those who once felt defeated by their challenge but are ready now to lighten their hearts and renew their passion for life. It is for those who need a reminder that every winter gives way to a new spring. It is for those who need a way to turn the ashes of an ending into the shoots of new personal growth.

You don't have to be of Italian heritage to glean valuable advice from this book, but it will resonate in anyone who has experienced some aspect of the Italian culture firsthand. The American adage "When life hands you lemons make lemonade" implies that we should accept and make the best of our struggles. That may be true, but it also sounds like a life sentence of "grin and bear it." After all, lemonade retains some of its bitterness despite the added sugar. The *limoncello* metaphor better describes how I prefer to face *my* challenges. If I really respect the nature of life—and death—I know that bitterness makes no sense. *Limoncello* (lemon liqueur) is made from the surprisingly sweet lemons found along the Amalfi Coast. There is no bitterness in this beverage but rather a bit of added kick, as in the kick that reminds me to get back up after defeat and make my life even better than before.

Over the years, I have studied and experienced certain aspects of Italian culture and observed remarkable exemplars of what it means to dust oneself off and "rise up singing" after adversity. In this book, I share the healing gift of my cultural heritage with you.

The Lemons into Limoncello Concept

The title for this book came to me one day while I was trudging up the steep, winding road that connects *Vettica Maggiore* (the section of Praiano, Italy, that embraces the sea) with its medieval counterpart on the mountain above. Suddenly, in the sweltering heat of a bright Italian sun, a little yellow blimp that was severed from its tree branch by the weight of its juices dropped before me. It seemed this proud Amalfi lemon refused to be passed by without due admiration. As I knelt to take a closer look, an elderly gentleman came walking, almost floating, toward me, with a cane that appeared more decorative than necessary hooked over his arm.

"*Che peccato* (What a shame)," I said. "This lemon is much too beautiful to go to waste, isn't it?"

The stranger cocked his head curiously.

"*Il li-mo-ne* (The lemon)," I enunciated, thinking he hadn't heard.

"*Ho sentito, ho sentito* (I heard you)," he replied. "*Ma scusa, perchè dovrà andare sprecato?* (But excuse me, why would it go to waste?)"

"Well, because it fell," I declared; as if it were a universal truth that you shouldn't eat fruit that has fallen to the ground.

Then, with a smile that made the Italian octogenarian boyishly chivalrous, he replied, "*Per favore* (Please), please hand me that lemon. I will bring it home to my wife. She turns lemons like these into *limoncello* (lemon liqueur)!"

Mind-set is everything when it comes to getting through hardship. The fallen lemon was by no means a disaster but rather a treasure to this gentleman, and a subtle reminder to me of how perception influences our reality. The Italian *arte d'arrangiarsi* (the art of getting by) is the belief in one's ability to get by, no matter what. It is a cultural assumption of confidence that we can all make it through anything. We can.

Italy's history of strife and victory, defeat and resurrection, has coalesced to form a culture that embraces complexity as naturally as it relishes simplicity. It is a nation whose people value wisdom and excellence as readily as they embrace life's requisite imperfections. By her cultural example, Italy teaches us to squeeze every drop of pleasure from a day, and "bank" our emotional resources so we can get through those inevitable rainy days of hardship.

The lemons-into-*limoncello* approach for getting through personal crisis was prompted by the experience of my own personal loss. Once my state of shock began to dissipate, I immersed myself in the readings of the Italian sages and made notes about the lifestyle wisdom I learned from years of observing Italian family members, colleagues, and friends. They softened the blows of their own hardship with simple yet consistent feel-good rituals. They used creativity and courage to build a bridge that extended into an enlightened new phase of life. The wisdom and traditions of my heritage gave me comfort and clarity, and the kind of healing that allowed me to eventually renew my life. I don't mean to say it was easy. Major loss changes us forever. But we don't have to let loss keep us from turning the rest of our life into a masterpiece.

My lemons-into-*limoncello* recipe for moving forward after a personal crisis includes a cup of patience, a ladle of self-enhancing rituals, and a swirl of unwavering appreciation for the little treasures that show up to make us smile each day. *Lemons into Limoncello* is one approach that I hope will make a difference for you and give you the support and encouragement you need to go beyond just tolerating your post-loss existence to becoming a full participant in all of the wonders that await you right now.

How I Came to Write This Book

Marco Aurelio, the ancient Roman emperor and philosopher, wrote: "The art of life is more like the wrestler's art than the dancer's . . . we need to stand ready and firm to meet onsets which are sudden and unexpected."[1] Never was this truer for me than on the morning of November 14, 2008.

I had just stepped out of the shower and was waiting for Tom—my husband of thirty-two years—to bring me a towel from the dryer. That towel never came. The next thing I remember is desperately trying to revive his lifeless body, but hearing only the echo of an unmistakable death rattle from deep within a chest that was warm and breathing life just minutes before. It was a horror I could never have imagined and of such a magnitude that I could barely breathe myself.

No matter how natural a part of the life cycle, death still always comes as a shock. It only took one instant for life as I knew it to fall clear away. Tom had been my best friend since we were children making sand-castles on the beach where our parents once both had summer cottages. Through good and bad, we were always a team. I couldn't imagine how I would ever be able to go on without him. The suddenness of his death made it doubly difficult to process. A man so strong and healthy—how could this be?

A curious thing about personal tragedy—it doesn't discriminate. At one time or another, the road for all of us gets rocky, sometimes impossibly so, it seems. The wisdom I drew from my cultural roots felt like a steady hand guiding me gently forward, refusing to let me remain stuck forever in my sorrow.

Life Goes On—As It Should

I now come back from walking my dog to the familiar aroma of bubbling tomato and basil sauce. The traditions of my childhood are like a sure-footed embrace from my ancestors. I travel momentarily back to my grandmother's kitchen, where I would stand alongside her on a Sunday morning as she stirred the pot of tomato sauce infused with freshly browned meatballs and hand-stuffed sausage. This sensation keeps me grounded, calm, and reassured. The Italian customs I continue to maintain provide me with stability when I feel off-balance.

Life ultimately is like an ancient mosaic, the kind that once lined the inner hallways in almost every Roman home. At short range you can distinguish the individual colors, shapes, and materials—shiny stone, rich lapis, malachite, colored glass. You might notice that many of the pieces have been chipped, weathered, or dulled, just like the glitches in our lives. Yet despite the "wounded" pieces, when you step back you are still captivated by the overall wholeness of an image that makes perfect sense. Personal resilience comes from taking a step back from our troubles and focusing on the broader experience. Life still holds its share of joy, even when you experience the opposite.

My survival template is rooted in the simple traditions and wisdom of my Italian cultural heritage. The ritualistic act of making Sunday morning tomato sauce can be deeply therapeutic in the "old world" tradition. I plunge an end of my crusty Italian bread into my homemade marinara and *fare la scarpetta* (make a little "shoe" out of bread, to be filled with sauce), which is one of my favorite feel-good rituals. Pavarotti's "Nessun Dorma" plays in the background, and I let the lyrics confirm what my heart has already affirmed: *All'alba vincerò, vincerò, vincerò* (At dawn I will win, I will win, I will win). In fact, I feel I have won. I have won back a renewed zest for life through the same techniques I will share with you in this book. Trust in the new dawn that awaits you, too.

Layout of the Book

This book is divided into four sections, or *parti*, that very closely follow the way a person builds resilience after loss. Part I, *Lascia Stare*, helps you deal with the initial phase of your loss by giving you permission to do nothing other than adjust to what has happened. You will discover how faith, music, the sweetness of doing nothing, and giving yourself daily gifts of simple joy will help cushion your blow. Part II, *Pian Piano,* is about going slowly but surely forward into a brighter, new phase of life. Here I encourage you to begin to surround yourself with the uplifting power of beauty. I ask you to simplify your surroundings, to begin to plan small comforting rituals into each day. To feed your mind, I suggest you turn to the sages, to prepare for the necessary letting-go phase (which we all must do in order to move ahead). Part III, *Reagire,* gives you the courage to take action on a larger scale toward renewing your life. Decluttering your house, your car, and your office will create space for what is important. Putting some of your tasks on "automatic pilot" will help you conserve energy, and you will discover how immersing yourself in physical work will distract you enough to heal the emotions. It is also time now to build a community. You can start by becoming a regular someplace where "everybody knows your name." Part IV, *Andare Avanti!* is about going forward with passion and enthusiasm into your brand-new life. Taking care of your health Italian-style, including a Mediterranean diet upon which so much research is based, will help you stay physically strong and vibrant. To strengthen your emotional resources you must have the right thoughts, one of which consists of thinking of each morning as a new opportunity to live life to the fullest. Of course nothing makes you feel better than a head-to-toe Italian makeover. Doing a frenzied dance, such as the traditional tarantella, can help evoke laughter once again, and you should do it often and with all of your heart. Finally, your creativity at this stage represents a more authentic expression of who you are and will allow you to share your unique gifts with the world.

Now it is time to start your own feel-good rituals. I invite you to begin with my Sunday morning sauce tradition, if you are so inclined. Don't forget to dunk the end of your Italian bread and *fare la scarpetta* to test the seasonings!

D'Agostino's Tomato and Basil Sauce

MAKES ENOUGH FOR A ONE-POUND BOX OF PASTA

2–3 tablespoons extra-virgin olive oil

2–4 cloves garlic (depending on your tastes), finely minced

Sprinkle of red pepper flakes (according to how spicy you like your sauce)

1 28-ounce can San Marzano tomatoes

Generous handful fresh basil, chopped

Handful fresh Italian parsley, chopped

Splash of balsamic vinegar

Splash of good table wine (either red or white—whatever you have open)

Salt, pepper, and dried oregano to taste

Pour just enough oil to coat the bottom of an enamel saucepot and heat on medium. When the oil is heated, add the garlic and red pepper flakes. Just as the garlic begins to turn golden, add the tomatoes. Raise the heat in order to bring to a boil, then stir and lower the heat to a simmer. Add the remaining ingredients, including fresh herbs, vinegar, wine, and seasonings. Loosely cover the pot, leaving about a ½-inch slit for steam to evaporate so the sauce can thicken. Stir occasionally, leaving the pot to simmer for approximately two hours. This will make sauce for one pound of pasta, just the right amount for a wonderful first course for a family gathering. If you prefer a nice meat flavoring, you can add browned sausage and meatballs, and let them finish cooking in the sauce.

Creating a regular ritual that makes you feel good—whether making a pot of tomato sauce every Sunday or declaring movie night with friends every Friday—will acclimate you to the reality that life still holds joy, things to look forward to, and ways to lighten the burden of your sadness.

Buon appetito (Eat well)!

Parte Prima (Part I)

Lascia Stare:
Just Let It Be . . .
for Now

Essere Credente:
Believe in Something Greater

Se non fai silenzio dentro di te, non puoi sentire la voce di Dio [1]
If you don't create silence inside of you, you will not be
able to hear God's voice.
—Valerio Albisetti

L A BASILICA DI SANTA MARIA IN TRASTEVERE is one of the oldest
churches in Rome and dates back to possibly the third century,
when Christianity was still a minority religion. Its visual beauty
has been enriched from the subsequent modifications and addi-
tions throughout the centuries. There is a magnificent gilded altar and
ceiling mosaics that give the feeling of a sacred glow or a soothing halo.
The ancient tomb pieces embedded into the walls and the geometric
mosaic tiled floors give testimony to a devotion to God from the beginning of time. The saintly relics lend a mysticism that give hope and

reaffirm faith. At the feet of a lifelike sculpture of San Antonio (a saint known for granting wishes) are snowfalls of prayer requests, to which I added mine. The peaceful awe of this sacred setting floods my senses with tranquility. One thing I love best about the culture of my heritage is that religious faith plays a major role. In Italian life, religion is more an experience than a mere adherence to dogma. Ever present is a reverence for life and for God as its creator. Faith reassures believers that no matter what unsettling changes we must face across our lifetime, there is a powerful force that will always remain eternal and unchanging. Most Italians call that force *"Il Signore,"* God.

Research confirms the capacity of faith to help us overcome personal crisis. Researchers from the Istituto di Fisiologia Clinica del CNR di Pisa reported that praying and having an active faith in God may increase our odds of survival in a health crisis. In this study, 179 liver transplant patients at the University of Pisa were followed for four years after their operations. After controlling for age, sex, level of education, possible complications from surgery, and types of liver disease, they found that those who stated they were not religious had a three times greater risk of mortality than those who had a strong faith in God—no matter what religion they ascribed to.[2] One participant put it this way: *"Ho fede in Dio, sono ancora vivo grazie a Lui. La Sua vicinanza mi sta rendendo più forte e tranquillo.* (I have faith in God, I am still living thanks to Him. His close presence makes me stronger and more tranquil.)" A generic belief in "destiny" did not have the same survival effects, according to an article reported about this study in the Italian daily newspaper *Il Corriere della Sera.*[3]

In contemporary American culture, we seem to have forsaken belief in God in exchange for a belief in crystals, arbitrary concepts of "spirit," or commercialized ancient rituals (for example, sweat lodges) that we blindly follow even though we know little about their origins. *Il Corriere della Sera* reported that forty-two additional studies involving 126,000 people found evidence that religiosity correlated to longevity. Renowned Italian writer Umberto Eco noted, "When men stop believing in God, it isn't that they then believe in nothing: They believe in everything."[4] That belief in "everything" and anything will not help us get through our crises the way a solid belief in God will. This isn't to say that you must follow my concept of God; in fact, you should follow your own. If you feel guilty because you hadn't thought about your faith until crisis hit—don't. Consider this a new day and a step closer to your personal reawakening.

Though the particulars of my own spiritual beliefs have waxed, waned, and morphed over the years, I can tell you without hesitation that my belief in God has always held firm, perhaps in spite of myself. What God looks like or sounds like, I don't really know. I never blame *Il Signore* for my losses; but I may call on Him to help me get through them. And one way or another, I do. Believing in the existence of a power greater than yourself can alleviate some of the burden of personal trauma and help you to feel like you don't have to go it alone.

Italians rely on their faith to help them get through life's ups and downs, regardless of whether or not they attend Holy Mass. According to a recent European Values Survey, 90 percent of Italians believe in God or some spirit force.[5] When it comes to getting through your most trying times, it really doesn't matter which religion you follow as long as you allow your faith to sustain you, keep you hopeful, and help you to move out of your crisis and into the joy of living again. Believe in your heart that there is a God who will guide you out of your temporary dark tunnel.

Read Religiously for Fifteen Minutes a Day

In *Religious Reading: The Place of Reading in the Practice of Religion*, author Paul J. Griffiths writes: "Reading religiously, I've come to think, is central to being religious."[6] What we read on a regular basis—just like any other habitual behaviors we engage in—becomes part of our identity. For those of you who despair about not being able to fully feel the presence of some concept of God in your life, regular reading of religious text may help that to change, if you are open to the possibility.

If you read about different faiths, you will notice some universal principles that probably guide your own values, behaviors, and attitudes. It has never been acceptable in any faith to kill or mistreat others, or denigrate the image of God. Through these readings, you will also discover insightful passages and stories that sustain you in difficult times.

I don't want to give you the impression that Italians carry bibles around in their pockets or quote scriptures in everyday conversation. Yet, with regularity, almost every Italian in my life either has a saint he or she feels close to or can produce a parable or passage that has brought solace when life got tough.

For example, Gianpaolo, who was baptized and raised Catholic, was always drawn to the Old Testament. His love of those readings in his youth prompted him to explore Jewish services and read the Torah regularly. I began to see a change in his self-confidence and the way he carried himself, though he never proselytized. Religion is, after all, personal. Gianpaolo's real test came when he brought his family to a camping site off the coast of southern Rome and his young son was mauled by a vicious dog; half of the flesh on this young boy's face was torn off. Gianpaolo was standing close by, but the attack happened so fast that he was unable to intervene and prevent the injuries. Unable to forgive himself for what he felt was a fundamental duty of a father to protect, his self-admonishments tortured him until he reconnected to his regular scripture reading. Each night, whenever thoughts of guilt or despair crept in, he opened his Old Testament and reread the passages that by then had become like familiar friends.

His son has since had plastic surgery to repair his facial features and received damages from his legal suit to pay for the interventions. Gianpaolo has restored peace in his life, and he and his son are back to swimming, camping, woodworking, and doing all of the things they love together. Life is good, and he admits that his regular religious readings helped him to let go of his self-condemnation and refocus on what was more important—being fully present for his son's recovery.

Find Your Style of Daily Prayer

In the more remote towns of Italy, people are quick to admit that prayer can be useful. When there is not enough rain for the crops, whole communities might gather to pray. Eventually the rain comes. Does it come because of the prayer, or because of the power of prayer to help one persevere patiently? The more important question is: Does the distinction even matter?

I have always loved stepping out of the bright sunlight and into the semidarkness of a quiet Italian church in the middle of the day. Inevitably, there are one or two elderly women whispering Hail Marys as a hint of colored light bounces off their rosary beads, and deep-red and blue glass candles flicker with hopeful intentions. Just being in this setting begets tranquility. It provides a safe and necessary space for reflection and emotional regrouping.

Prayer can also help push out more troubling thoughts that assault you. *How will I make it without this person? How will I survive after my layoff becomes final? How will I ever find another place to live? This disease will only get worse; I will never feel good again.* Keeping your thoughts occupied with prayer provides momentary relief from worry and grief. Any time you can counter panic with calm, you can avoid becoming overwhelmed by your grief.

The style of prayer that clicks for you is personal. When going through trauma, you may find comfort in reciting traditional prayers, like this classic peace Prayer of St. Francis of Assisi:

Prayer of Saint Francis of Assisi

Lord, make me an instrument of Thy peace.
Where there is hatred, let me bring love.
Where there is injury, let me bring pardon.
Where there is discord, let me bring union.
Where there is doubt, let me bring faith.
Where there is error, let me bring truth.
Where there is despair, let me bring hope.
Where there is sadness, let me bring joy.
Where there is darkness, let me bring light.
Grant that I may not so much seek
to be consoled as to console,
to be understood as to understand,
to be loved as to love.

For it is in giving that we receive.

It is in pardoning that we are pardoned.

It is in dying that we are born to eternal life.

Journaling and Free-Form Prayer

While reciting formal prayer has its advantages (repetition can be quite calming), prayer can also be a free-form conversation with God, either verbally or as a written journal. Research psychologist James Pennebaker found that journaling is therapeutic, and merely writing down your thoughts about the trauma you have gone through can be effective.[7] Writing about stressful events helps us to better cope with those events and can reduce the stress that leads to physical illness. When you have been assaulted by a trauma, your life seems like it was plunged into chaos: There may be people coming around to offer help, calls from bill collectors if you haven't had the presence of mind to pay your bills for a period, errands that are waiting for you that you don't have the energy to complete. Everything will work out. Remember, for now, all you need do is *lascia stare* (let it be). Start small by writing just a few words each night in your journal to reaffirm your faith that a loving God will help you to get through.

Here is a sample journal entry to help you get started. You can customize to resonate with your current situation.

Dear God,

Today as I think about _____ (my loss) _____, I feel _____.

I want to be able to find peace inside myself and feel joy once again. Please show me the way to heal and find light from this darkness. Guide me in the new direction where I am now meant to be. Help me let go of the past, accept my new reality, and become wiser, kinder, and more fully present in the gift of life that I have been given. Help me to forgive myself for any past mistakes as I work toward a more positive mind-set and healthier body from this day on. Thank you for the gift of life. I know you are by my side.

Frequent a Place of Worship

Mariagiovanna lost both her husband and daughter to the same genetic disease. While she was taking care of one who lay dying, the other became ill and was diagnosed with the same fatal disease. She became frantic in her state of emergency as she tirelessly cared for her two loved ones, all the while knowing she would soon lose the two people she loved most. After the devastation of her double tragedy, Maria decided to become more involved in a church she had been estranged from for many years. She started to attend Mass regularly again and found great comfort in the community aspect of the services and events. Through the church's charity projects she poured her grief energy into volunteer work alongside other church members, and every day was able to see how she could make a difference in the neighborhoods that needed her. She cooked and brought meals to those who couldn't get out, visited sick children to whom she would read stories, and took seniors to their doctors' appointments when they weren't otherwise able to get there. This didn't take away her sorrow, but it did give her a sense of greater purpose so she wouldn't have to be defined by that sorrow.

Sometimes, attending different religious services may increase your chances of hearing just the right words you need at the time you most need to hear them. Houses of worship can also be visited during the day for quiet solitude and renewal from the stress and noise you are extra-sensitive to right now.

Explore Religious Artifacts

There is nothing new about the use of religious artifacts. Throughout history, artifacts have given people something concrete to relate to visually, olfactorally, or tactually. This is true across cultures, not just in the Italian culture. Religious artifacts also serve as important symbols of hope and redemption.

When I was growing up, it was commonplace to be surrounded by rosary beads, statues, crosses, incense, and holy water. Some may see these as crutches; but for others they serve as a source of comfort in difficult times.

Holy images also have a strong presence in traditional Italian homes. It is common to find reproductions of classic religious paintings on the walls in various rooms throughout the house. Even the SITA bus that scurries up and down the Amalfi Coast, hugging the edge of the lemon tree–dotted hillside many times a day at what might seem to the foreigner a breakneck speed, has a picture of the Blessed Virgin Mary in front of the driver. It is a symbol of reassurance that the ride will proceed safely, despite how things look. Religious artifacts serve as concrete symbols of faith and as reminders that some force outside of this world—and much stronger than us—will help to get us by.

How Religious Artifacts
Can Support You During Crisis

If the idea resonates with you, think about selecting a religious artifact to carry in your purse or pocket. Consider it your powerful little reminder that things will be all right and that you are not alone. Some people carry a rabbit's foot, a lucky stone, or a four-leaf clover. A religious artifact, however, symbolizes "something greater," which takes the pressure off you to control everything that happens in life. You may find this practice gives you strength. Here are some ways to start:

- ✓ Go to a religious store or find one online. Browse the images, statues, prayer beads, relics, jewelry, and plaques. You may be drawn to a certain object more than others. That is the one to purchase.
- ✓ Keep your artifact in your purse or pocket every day, or close by on your desk or kitchen counter where you will see it and be able to touch it often.
- ✓ Whenever you touch your artifact, repeat the words, "I am at peace. I am getting through my loss, and my life is still filled with goodness."

Adopt a Saint and You'll Never Be Alone

Saints have a special place in Italian life. Saints are virtuous figures who in many cases overcame terrible suffering, illness, or torture, or lived exemplary lives of giving to others and performing miracles. Because saints were once human beings who lived on earth and suffered many of the same struggles we deal with in our own lives, they are thought to understand what we are going through. They have compassion for our suffering. They inspire us and serve as our bridge to life everlasting.

Everyone in the Italian family has a *onomastico* (name saint), and every Italian town is protected by a patron saint. There is a saint for every medical condition and every occupation. St. Christopher used to sit on our dashboards to protect us on the drive home. Whenever we lost something, a prayer to St. Anthony repeated three times would usually help us find it. We read about unforgettable examples of courage, kindness, and determination in the lives of the saints. I am not a theologian, but I do like the idea of saints. We can't see them, but it is nice to think there are heavenly beings who are in our corner and by our side to help get us through the most challenging of times. Because saints are a given in the lives of most Italians, they never feel alone.

A basic Internet search will easily pull up a list of saints and what they represent. I've always loved March 19, when my family celebrated the feast of San Giuseppe, St. Joseph's Day. It came only two days after the more commercialized St. Patrick's Day festivities. In Italy, San Giuseppe is Father's Day, as Joseph was the father of Jesus.

Read up on saints and find one for your name, town, or situation. When you find a special saint who has meaning for you, learn about his or her story and ask that saint to protect you and stand by you as you face the changes brought about by your crisis. In the Italian Catholic tradition there are saints for life, miracles, the elderly, employment, finances, prosperity, cancer, dogs, illness, and much more. You can identify with more than one saint as your situation changes. St. Rita is the patron saint of loneliness. St. Paul, because of his epistolary contribution to the New Testament, is considered the patron saint of writers. St. Francis of Assisi is the patron of animals. You can always find a saint with whom you can identify. Saints can become your network of support, too, even if you choose to think of them as mere inspirational, historical figures and nothing more.

To me, faith is not about mathematical equations and empirical data. It is about claiming the resources we need to transcend our darkest hour. Learning about saints and how their stories relate to yours can be a source of support for you, too.

Meditate at Least Five Minutes per Day

For many, meditation is similar to prayer. It is more secular, and a viable alternative if the idea of religious faith does not appeal to you. Meditation has also been shown to improve blood flow to the parts of the brain responsible for anxiety and depression. It helps you bring your heart and mind back "home" when it wanders out to grief and worry. At a recent conference in Lucca, Nitamo Montecucco, professor of psychosomatics at the University of Milan, stated, "Positive emotions are a way of life, which we can attain through the ancient path of meditation, which affects neurotransmitters, stimulates the immune system, decreases inflammation, and gives us a sense of inner peace."[8]

In conducting meditation workshops for a Yale cardiac study, I encourage my participants to take time to meditate each day on their own—even five or ten minutes once or twice a day if that is all they have. They often tell me that this practice has made a significant difference in their tranquility. Brain researcher Dr. Daniel Amen recommends just twelve minutes of consistent daily meditation time in order to see positive physical changes in the brain.[9] Ten to twelve minutes of chanting, mantra, visualization, or silent meditation can also be a wonderful healing tool to get you through adversity. Like any positive habit, you should give your meditation practice at least twenty-one days to become a habit. Here is how to start:

1. Sit comfortably but upright in a place where there will be no interruptions for at least five minutes. Turn off your cell phone and other electronic devices. Shut the door if you are in your home or office, and ask others to respect this time.

2. Begin by imagining yourself sitting in a gorgeous, fragrant lemon grove on Italy's Amalfi Coast (you can do an image search on your favorite search engine beforehand and find many beautiful photos of Italian lemon groves). I like the photos that show the sun's rays streaming through a covering of lush green leaves, with plump yellow balls hanging from the arbor.

3. As you imagine yourself sitting in the cool grass beneath the lemon grove, feel the warmth of the sun on your shoulders. Let your skin soak in that soothing warmth. A gentle sea breeze from the Gulf of Salerno brushes against your cheeks. As you inhale, the sweet smell of ripe lemons fills your nostrils and awakens your lungs. You have no worries, no cares, for this moment you are one with the peace and safety of this scene.

4. Take a deep, slow breath through your nose. Hold it for a few seconds, then gently exhale through your mouth. Do a few more rounds of this slow breathing cycle, and, as you do, let the clean oxygenated air circulate through your entire body. Feel your stomach and diaphragm puff out as you inhale. Feel your belly contract again toward your spine as you exhale.

5. Now let your breathing come to normal, and, while visualizing the beauty of the lemon grove that surrounds you, repeat the word *peace* to yourself. *Peace. Peace.* With every exhalation. If other thoughts intrude, just acknowledge them and let them go. Imagine intruding thoughts floating out into the sky in a helium balloon. You are at peace. Continue for five minutes.

At the end of the meditation you may find that even more than five minutes have gone by, but at least start with the five. It is brief enough to let your body and mind become used to this new habit, and it does need to become a habit for you to reap the benefits. Practice this meditation each day upon awakening or at bedtime to help you calm your mind so you can get to sleep. Let it be the first of many regular gifts you give to yourself.

Loss and trauma take away your confidence. The more you complete acts of good self-care like taking meditation breaks, the more your confidence and self-esteem will start to return. Inner peace will begin to take root in your heart and create a solid foundation for your complete healing and personal renaissance.

Let Faith Carry You Through

✓ Read sacred text.
✓ Pray daily or journal.
✓ Join or visit a place of worship.
✓ Use religious artifacts.
✓ Learn about the saints.
✓ Meditate.

2

Musica è . . .
Let Music Lift You Up

The essence of music is to harmonize and heal.
—Piero Ferrucci, author of *Beauty and the Soul*

ANDREA BOCELLI, WHO HAS GLAUCOMA, once told an interviewer that when he was a child, his mother comforted him by playing classical records. He developed his love of opera this way. Even after losing his sight completely in a soccer accident at the age of twelve, he went on to eventually fulfill his dream to become a singer and was discovered by the great Pavarotti.

"I believe that the obstacles God gives us to overcome are in proportion to the strengths and abilities he gives us to overcome them," said Bocelli.[1] Music helped Bocelli triumph over his challenges, and now, through the music he makes for us, we can do the same. Listen to his version of "*Canto Della Terra*" ("Song of the Earth"), which reminds us of how beautifully the world keeps turning, giving us the mighty sun.

Even if you don't understand the words, you will be moved by the crescendos and diminuendos of his vocals, not dissimilar to the way grief waxes and wanes when you move through loss. You can feel how certain music affects your mood.

Music may also have a positive effect on your physical well-being, something most people neglect in the initial stages of a personal crisis or loss. This was shown in the work of Dr. Mike Miller, a cardiology researcher at the University of Maryland Medical Center in Baltimore, who was profiled in a recent CNN health blog. Miller tested the effects on the heart of either playing music or simply listening to it. He discovered that music we relate to or that makes us feel good actually opens up the heart's blood vessels and produces chemicals that are protective to the heart. On the other hand, when listening to music we don't like, the vessels begin to close up, and over time can have a damaging effect on cardiovascular health. Music is a powerful tool when you are working through feelings of loss and anxiety.

Challenges that would exasperate the average person used to make one of my Italian cousins sing. He told me once that misfortune gives us two choices: We can cry or we can sing till we no longer feel like crying. When coping with a major personal crisis, even the smallest additional thing that goes wrong can push your emotions over the edge.

When You Are Going Through Crisis, Start Singing

Singing can help you avoid feeling overwhelmed. In the days following the death of my husband, if any part of my day went wrong, even something as minute as the house key not fitting smoothly into the door lock, I would become so agitated that I would either try to jam it in or throw the entire key chain on the ground and give up. It seemed like I had no resources left to cope with additional challenges. Then I bought a little iPod, filled it with the familiar Italian songs I grew up with, and discovered that a little bit of the right music gave me the patience required to deal with those ancillary minor glitches that would spring up during my bereavement. On the other hand, I noticed that if a car came down the street blasting bass and violent lyrics, I would feel irritated and on edge. You may have noticed that the type of music that reaches your ears directly influences your mood, too.

You can turn your mood around with a simple positive song, even if you only sing it to yourself. As I laugh at my own attempts at singing, I remember not to take things too seriously. Sometimes song helps me cope with the little things, so I have more energy to better cope with the bigger things. Song represents lightheartedness and hope. While singing is the last thing you may feel like doing when you are going through loss, it is important to do it anyway, even if you start with a hum. Hum or sing through your smaller frustrations and the lightheartedness produced by the melody will help you conserve the emotional energy you need to process your loss.

Match the Music to What You Need Most

Some people need to avoid music that triggers painful memories of their loss. If, for example, you just lost your sister and the two of you shared the same favorite song, at first hearing that song following your loss could be more painful than restorative. Honor your instincts. You will be able to listen to it someday again, and even listen with new appreciation for the connection to her. In the "let it be" stage, however, you need all of your psychic (mental) energy to recoup and regroup. You don't need any additional triggers for emotional pain. In contrast, other people need to hear that "memory" music right away to help them release their emotions and have a good cry. Using music as a catharsis is fine, too, if it makes you feel better afterward. Try playing a happy song to get some needed relief from your grief, or escape whatever you are dealing with entirely for a few moments. Try listening to something you've never heard before, a piece that helps distract you from your woes for a couple of minutes but whose melody and rhythm make you feel peaceful. *Ah, la bella musica!* Beautiful music is an effective antidote to misery.

When you need self-forgiveness. Loss sometimes brings about guilt and self-doubt. *Had I only taken her to the doctor sooner, she may have survived. Had we only moved out to Arizona when the company offered me a transfer, I wouldn't be out of work now. Had we only chosen the smaller home with more affordable payments, we wouldn't be buried in debt now with our home in foreclosure.*

Excessive guilt imprisons us in our own hell on earth. Joseph, whose son doesn't speak to him over an argument they had ten years ago, blames himself. Bad enough that his son is punishing him; on top of that, Joseph punishes *himself* daily by perseverating on different things he could have said to head off the fight. Theresa, who lost a friendship when she asked for the money she had loaned her friend to be returned, blames herself for even having asked for it back.

Self-forgiveness is one of the most important ways we can help ourselves through loss. Music can help grievers with unresolved forgiveness issues.[3] Our energy is more productively spent in resolving to do better from here on in and let go of self-loathing. Music can help you let go

of your self-punishing thoughts and forgive yourself as you would forgive your children for their mistakes. Listen to music that will inspire,
soothe, encourage, and even cry with you. Let the melody wash over
your emotional wounds and heal them like the ocean's healing salt
water. Let it help you forgive yourself.

Here is how. Make a list of songs whose lyrics most express the feelings you have surrounding your loss. Even music with sad lyrics can
make you feel supported and confirm you are not alone. This is different
from music that stresses you out.

Choose the music for its message. *"Mi manchi"* ("I Miss You") is
a beautiful ballad sung by Bocelli about someone who misses another
so much that the heart is breaking while the singer goes through the
motions of an otherwise normal life. A song like this one reflects the
simple purity of an open heart that loves. There doesn't have to be a
resolution or a happy ending for music to help you to forgive yourself.
A compelling melody, even if the words are in another language, may
also be effective. You can also experiment with making your own music
and writing out the lyrics, the words you wish to say to the loved one
you miss. If you play an instrument, you might play a song and dedicate
it to your loved one.

**Let the music you surround yourself with keep bringing you to
a better place.** Let the music you expose yourself to each day begin
to lift your spirits and fill the void caused by your loss. You can select
music that acknowledges your sadness, your courage, your hope, and
your strength. After going through a painful divorce when her husband left her for his young secretary, Jayelle played two songs to help
her get through her anguish and back into life: Tony Bennett's "I Won't
Cry Anymore" and Frank Sinatra's "New York, New York." Both have

a message of good things to come. "I Won't Cry Anymore" is about a man whose love has left him. While acknowledging his broken heart, he has also resolved to end his tears, accept reality, and move on. When Jayelle listened to this song, it felt as if she had a friend who really understood what she was going through. "New York, New York" is, of course, about a place you can go to make your dreams come true. What a life-affirming message, that so many wonders still await you. Don't give up. *Never* lose heart!

When you need hope. Claudio Monteverdi, best known for writing *Orfeo* (one of the first operas), believed that the purpose of all music is to affect the soul. His genius shone in the way he used words, harmony, and rhythm to touch his audiences. The primary emphasis was on text—story line and poetry set to music. His opera *L'incoronazione di Poppea* (*The Coronation of Poppea*) combined tragic, romantic, and comedic scenes in the same opera—a realistic snapshot of how our lives really are. In listening to a piece like this, we are reminded that life is not only about the tragedy: It is also about the laughter, love, and hope.

When you feel weighed down by your sadness and grief, sometimes a simple instrumental can feel like a healing salve to a wounded heart. Sometimes we just need a vacation from words when making our way out from personal crisis. The violin, when played well, is considered by many to be the musical instrument closest to a human voice. This instrument evokes much of the same emotion that a good vocal does. *Phantasticus: 17th Century Italian Violin Music* is a CD with several pieces that will surely lift a low spirit. One of my favorites is Pandolfi's Violin Sonata, op. 4, no. 3, "*La Monella Romanesca,*" but there are several others that will coax an aching heart to peacefulness. For a list of my suggestions, visit http://raeleenmautner.com.

Try other instrumentals, too, like the music of a cello or saxophone. Rocco Ventrella is a popular contemporary, Bari-born musician who plays sax and clarinet with equal mastery. "Soulful Strut" on his album *Give Me the Groove* is something that makes perfect background sound when you are feeling sluggish and need some motivation to get up again and get moving. Gifted trumpeter Chris Botti, who spent part of his childhood in Italy, plays an exquisite version of "*Ave Maria*" that can be found on his album *Italia*, a collection of songs dedicated to his Italian roots. The album also includes a song he performs as accompaniment to the vocals of Andrea Bocelli.

When you need God. Chants, gospel, and other sacred music have been used for centuries to induce a meditative state. Sacred music can become the prayer you feel too confused to compose yourself. The contemplative and soothing quality of sacred music, such as some of the vespers and oratorios of Alessandro Scarlatti, can give rest and relief to frazzled emotions.

In the initial period of my loss, I turned to Gregorio Allegri's *Miserere mei, Deus*. This sacred musical prayer began to soften the sharpness of my suffering. Composed for use in the Sistine Chapel in the late 1600s, the piece was based on Psalm 51, which begins "Have Mercy on Me, Oh God." I also felt a soulful connection to Zucchero's more earthy rendition of *Miserere*, which seemed a sacred plea to return to a state where life could once again be celebrated.

Francesco Petrarch, often called the Father of Humanism, wrote: "Man has no greater enemy than himself." When you are going through personal trauma, don't deprive yourself of music. Don't be your own enemy. You are worthy and deserving of joy, hope, and happiness. Give your heart what it needs.

When you need resilience. Music therapists are now employed in hospitals, nursing homes, rehabilitation centers, prisons, and schools because music has the power to soothe, stimulate, support, and even heal certain conditions. Researchers have found that bright and cheerful music (like that of Vivaldi) can reduce depression up to 25 percent and leave you feeling more optimistic and positive.[4] Music also appears to reduce the stress hormone cortisol.[5] When I first listened to Vivaldi's "Spring" (you will recognize the melody, even if you never knew its title), I went from being practically unable to get out of bed (when a person is sad, the whole world seems to come to a stop), to getting back onto my feet and poking around in my kitchen, to making a meal. It motivated me to start cooking again, and even wanting to get back outside and into the world.

If opera resonates with you, here is something to think about. As Leopold Fechtner used to joke, "The opera is a place where a man can get beaten to a pulp, and instead of dying, he rises up singing."[6] Music does make us feel like getting back in the game. I still listen to Pavarotti's "*Nessun Dorma*" (from Puccini's *Turandot*) as if it were Puccini's personal gift to me: "*All'alba vincerò, vincerò, VINCERÒ!*" ("At dawn I will win, I will win, I will win!") This is like a positive affirmation put to Italian musical notation. It really does work.

When you need to laugh. Comedy has been found in Italian music for centuries. In contemporary times, even political satire makes people laugh through song. Roberto Benigni, who starred as the protagonist in the Italian film *La Vita è Bella* (also popular in the United States under the title *Life Is Beautiful*) recorded an irreverently funny song called "Quando Penso a Berlusconi" ("When I think of Berlusconi"). The song gives a comedic look at what some Italians considered to be

former Prime Minister Silvio Berlusconi's gaffes, a
illustrious and dignified Italian history. The song
is another song sure to pull you from a slump of s
all positive emotions, is good for the heart and good for your i........
mind.

Get Reacquainted with Your Radio

Aside from music, there are other sounds that can be therapeutic. Years ago, a good friend from Milano gave me a shortwave radio for my birthday that enthralled me. At night before I went to bed, I could listen to voices all over the world come through in their native languages. That one little switch brought me to Italy, Germany, Russia, and France. I realized that no matter what was happening in my life, I was not the only person facing what I was going through; I was only one little speck out of millions on the globe.

Years later, I became a radio personality so that I, too, could have a positive effect on listeners. I wanted to be that voice that speaks to the lonely, the suffering, the grieving, the self-defeated. I wanted to broadcast positive radio that gets the message out that no matter what life hands us, there is light on the other end of that tunnel. Radio can help a lot during the initial stages of loss. You can turn the dial to the "feelgood" music of your childhood or some great talk radio. Italian inventor Guglielmo Marconi and others dedicated their lives to bequeathing us the excitement of radio. One way to tap into that pleasure is to listen in to my own radio show, "The Art of Living Well," from anywhere in the world. Just go to my website and click on the "radio" tab: http://raeleen mautner.com.

Nonna Angelina's old-fashioned Italian radio was the center of her verse. She would bustle about the kitchen accompanied by emotionally touching songs in Neapolitan dialect, such as "*Te Voglio Ben Assaje*" ("I Love You So Very Much"), sung by Sergio Bruni. She loved even the newscasts, because hearing them in familiar dialect was like hearing the voices of her people back home. While Angelina's music was just okay for me then, after Tom died I found that listening to Italian broadcasts like the ones she used to listen to made me feel like she was right back beside me. I imagined her cooking up a big batch of her lasagna and letting me know that everything was going to be all right.

I love Italian music from across the ages; but you should listen to any music that makes *you* feel good, that will get you back into life. Give yourself a regular daily dose of it by trying some of the following suggestions:

✓ Use music as background accompaniment to keep you calm and centered at home, in your car, or going for a walk. Take a few moments each day to just sit with your eyes closed and soak in a song you love.

✓ Feel surrounded and comforted by your ancestors: Make a list of songs and music they listened to, purchase some of those songs, and imagine while you listen that they are holding you in their strong arms and letting you know you will make it.

✓ Write down the names of songs you hear on the radio that make you feel good. Find those songs online and listen to them often.

✓ Consider making music yourself. Sing, even if off-key! Play an instrument that you haven't picked up in a while, or purchase one that you've always wanted to learn. Take a few lessons and get ready to let your life *move forward*.

Let the joy of music begin to lighten your heart and accompany you along the road to your personal renaissance. You are almost there!

Ways to Use Music to Heal

✓ Make a list of songs that make you feel good. Download them or listen on YouTube.

✓ Use beautiful music in the background as you go through your day.

✓ Choose music to change into a more positive mood.

✓ When small challenges pop up, choose to sing!

✓ Listen to music your ancestors used to listen to so you can feel them give you strength.

✓ Change the station when music that makes you feel stressed comes on.

✓ Listen to talk radio to distract you from your fears and worries.

3

Il Dolce Fare Niente:
Taste the Sweetness of
Doing Nothing

Non mi sembra un uomo libero quello che non ozia di tanto in tanto.[1]
It seems to me that a man is not really free if he can't laze around
now and then.

—Marco Tullio Cicerone

W HEN GIULIANA FIRST LOST HER FATHER, she would often sit out on her balcony with a cup of coffee and follow the trajectory of the ships gliding across the Gulf of Salerno with her eyes. *Il dolce fare niente* (the sweetness of doing nothing) is just as productive a time to Italians as is time doing something. Moments of "nothingness" are where one finds the space to reflect, acclimate to change, and accept the reality of major life transitions. Periodically pulling the plug on busyness is how Italians integrate loss into the richness of their life's tapestry. In a tapestry, you can't appreciate the beauty of lighter threads without the contrast of darker counterparts. Contrasts are what give us depth and insight.

I have a paper shredder that, after about fifteen minutes of shredding, shuts itself down to recharge. Try as I might, I can't force it to cut up even one more sheet until the mechanism decides *it* is ready to start working again. Although most of us would agree that our lives are much more important than a paper shredder, we often override what we know we need and push ourselves to exhaustion.

In the first few weeks following a major loss, your *only* job should be to acclimate to it so you can begin to heal. Accepting what has happened to you is no small task, yet it is a necessary one if you are to integrate the loss into your life. You need moments of silence to absorb the unfamiliarity that has entered your life and to come to terms with it. You need time to reexamine what will be meaningful to you from here on in, and to recharge your own battery much like the paper shredder needed to do. Give yourself permission to balance bursts of activity with periods of *il dolce fare niente* (the sweetness of doing nothing). Taking lots of "chill-out" breaks will help you store needed energy and regain resilience.

When I was a kid, my grandfather, Domenico, would water his little garden patch for what seemed like hours. Little mud pools would encircle our feet as the spray from the hose against the setting sun arched into a rainbow, then dissipated into thin air.

"Are we done yet?" I would ask, with an impatient tug at his sleeve. I wanted to go next door with him to buy a little glass bottle of grape soda at our friend Vito's package store.

No answer. I doubt he even heard me. *Giusto* (Just), he was right not to let me break his concentration. Domenico was clearly in another world, miles away. His everyday cares had already taken flight. As I got older and became a more careful observer, I realized that Nonno's endless garden-watering (*il dolce fare niente*) was his escape into serenity.

Inner tranquility is a byproduct of allowing for "downtime." Strategically placed pauses of nothingness can also open the door to the unexpected wonders of life that we might otherwise not notice. This reassures us that life is still good despite its difficulties. The sweetness of doing nothing relaxes the mind/body and creates an opportunity to just exist for right now. That is all you need to do. *Esistere,* just be.

Italians pay as much tribute to the practice of *il dolce fare niente* as they do to the privilege of working hard. Both are imperative for emotional and physical balance. In the movie *Eat, Pray, Love,* the barber scene was perhaps exaggerated but with some truth behind the humor: A client getting his hair cut is trying to explain to Julia Roberts's character that she needs a break from the hurriedness of American culture, where life is so busy that people need "reminders" to take a break from it all, as in the slogan "You Deserve a Break Today."[2] I'm sure you can think of others. And while this was meant to be funny, when you are going through loss, there is nothing funny about wearing yourself out trying to keep up your usual busy pace without stopping to process what has happened. Give yourself a break and avoid pushing yourself to exhaustion. Claim your right to regular pauses of repose and reflection, with no guilt attached.

Build Frequent Scioperi *(Strikes) into Your Life*

In Italy, one thing you can count on with regular frequency is the *sciopero* (strike), which often means a disruption in the flow of public transportation. Beneath smatterings of some colorful language when this happens, most Italians continue their day as if nothing out of the ordinary has happened. Politics aside, the frequency of the Italian *scioperi* almost seems like a built-in cultural reminder to break from the everyday *trantràn* (routine).

When you have incurred a major loss, panic and confusion often follow. The passage of time alone helps, as does what you do with that time. Letting the past distance itself and turning with gratitude toward an even brighter future requires unquestioning acceptance of reality. We can't keep assaulting our minds with worries, guilt, or fear. Nor can we push beyond the limited reserve of our physical energy. In a Huffington Post blog article, renowned physician Dr. Mark Hyman wrote, "Nothingness is the key to happiness." He discusses the inevitability of pain and human suffering, and how nothingness—or stillness—can help to break that cycle and reduce the impact of that suffering. He recommends just sitting in quietude and being mindful to the present moment.[3]

The impact of loss can be overwhelming. When Belinda's husband had to be admitted to a nursing home, she was frightened and worried. Bryan's prognosis wasn't good, and Belinda knew that from this point forward nothing would remain the same. A close friend told her to just take a few moments each day to sit still and "be" for a while. Belinda resisted this at first. She didn't have time to just sit still; there were endless things to do.

Belinda finally took her friend's advice the day she felt too frazzled to take another step. She began to schedule "rest" periods into the day at regular intervals. It didn't take long for her to look forward to them and to feel the effect of being refreshed. Soon she was able to calmly sit down and make a list of all the tasks that lay waiting. She made notes on how to find out about the way things worked if she needed more information. She gathered phone numbers of professionals who she could hire to do some of these tasks. Belinda even began to consider going back to school to finish a degree she had abandoned years ago. If it were not for giving herself the permission to engage in *il dolce fare niente*, she would have felt depleted. Instead, she now began to feel empowered.

We can't expect our bodies and minds to work 24/7 without restorative "shut-off" times. Not even in sleep do we get a guarantee for the kind of respite that comes from *il dolce fare niente*—a complete personal strike, where you think of nothing and do nothing (or at least as little as possible!). Give yourself permission to build a "do-nothing" half hour into each and every day. Consider the following ideas to help you get started:

When was the last time you . . .

✓ sat on a park bench in the middle of the day?

✓ lay on the grass and watched the clouds roll by?

✓ sat on the warm sand with your feet soaking in the cool ocean waves?

✓ stopped to inhale the sweet scent of a lilac blossom?

✓ watched clothes flapping dry in the wind on a clothesline?

✓ closed your eyes and listened to children playing outside?

✓ watered your garden and felt the spray cool your skin with its mist?

✓ observed how funny your little pet can be?

✓ put on some music and laid down with your eyes closed as you listened?

✓ cuddled up with someone (even a pet) that you love?

If you have not done at least three of the activities listed above since your loss, then it is urgent to make the sweetness of doing nothing a priority. Build it into your day habitually, just as regularly as you take your morning shower. You can take a few suggestions from the list above, or add to it with some soothing "nothingness" ideas of your own. Pleasure is good for you. It is healing. Your body will feel the effects almost immediately as you begin to care for yourself this way. The practice of doing nothing will refresh you throughout the day and give you the energy you need to embrace the changing landscape of your life.

Fare un Pisolino (Take a Nap)

Historically, in the Mediterranean where the climate is typically hot and dry, the afternoon siesta was seen as a necessity. *Il riposo Italiano* (the Italian rest) has been the long-held practice of closing one's store, going home to a delicious home-cooked meal, and taking a couple of hours to nap, relax, and recharge one's energy for use toward the remainder of the day. The *riposo,* or siesta, is a symbol for the Italian philosophy that quality of life takes precedence over making a few extra euro.[4] In Southern Italy especially, many small-shop owners still keep to this practice, as do banks and other places of business. But you don't need to live in Italy to take advantage of an afternoon nap routine. If you have taken some time off from work following your loss, you can easily declare a one-hour "do not disturb" naptime. Let well-meaning visitors know that between the hours of __ and __, you will neither be answering the door nor answering your phone. Even if you find it hard to sleep in the middle of the day, you can use a meditation tape with headphones, a relaxing sound maker, or a miniwaterfall. Some hypnosis tapes will put you to sleep quickly and soundly in next to no time.

If you are working, you can still take a ten- to fifteen-minute restorative nap or a short meditation break at your desk. My clients tell me it makes all the difference in the world on their mood. They feel stronger and more equipped to face the rest of the day. This is all about reclaiming your *gioia di vivere* (joy of living), one moment at a time.

Slow the Pace

I always advise people to slow the pace of their day by at least a half a beat. Slowing down physically helps your mind to wind down, too. When you are eating, for instance, pay attention to really savoring every forkful you bring to your lips. Close your eyes as you chew and really experience what you taste. Feel the texture on your tongue. Notice the sweetness of the beverage that passes your lips and flows down your throat. You will start to feel better almost immediately once you give yourself permission not to rush. Go slow. Take your time. Right now, the only thing that matters is *you*, not your "to-do" lists. Here are some additional ways to slow down:

- ✓ Get up a half hour early and take your time with your morning routine.
- ✓ Leave your house a full fifteen minutes earlier than you normally would for an appointment or for work. Now you don't have to worry if you run into traffic or road construction on your way.
- ✓ When you find yourself in a traffic jam or an exceptionally long line at the store, use the moment to do a 4–4–4. That is, inhale slowly through your nose to a count of four. Hold it, and let that life-giving oxygen circulate through your body to a count of four. Exhale through pursed lips to a slow count of four.
- ✓ Take the longer, but more scenic, route home instead of the highway. Speed is not of the essence anymore. Experiencing more enjoyable moments is.
- ✓ Practice the Lemons into *Limoncello* meditation found on my website, http://raeleenmautner.com.

O Sole Mio: Get Out and Get Sun

✓ Italians spend the majority of their day outdoors. This is true for both crowded city dwellers and rural inhabitants who need to get out and work the land. This lifestyle may also be responsible for the cheerful mood that many visitors notice when traveling through the *bel paese*, the beautiful country that is known as Italy.

✓ Following major loss, you may feel the "coldness" of unfamiliarity as your life changes. If you feel like a cold-blooded reptile, make it a point to get up and get some sun each day. Make sunlight a nonnegotiable survival tool if you want to feel better physically and emotionally. Try to get a brief walk outdoors in the early morning or late afternoon sun without sunscreen, as some doctors are now recommending. Let nature's warmth soothe you inside and out. Here are some additional suggestions.

✓ Get some indoor sunlight by relaxing next to a window and closing your eyes for a few moments. My grandmother loved to plant her rocking chair next to a sunny window on a cold winter afternoon. The only heat we had was from a small vent on an old-fashioned gas stove. Guiseppina would center herself square with the bright sun's rays, close her eyes, and gently rock back and forth letting the sun work its feel-good magic.

✓ On a nice day, get out and enjoy the colors of a flower garden. I remember that as a kid, I'd mindlessly watch the bees buzzing from flower to flower or a butterfly come to rest on one of the purple irises in the garden. These were moments for total restoration of the mind and spirit. When we got back to our day we'd be happy and smiling. Go out and just enjoy the colors of your own garden, or find a local park that has a botanical section and enjoy.

✓ If you are in an office all day, take your lunch break outside if your company has an outdoor seating area. Make sure to take frequent outdoor breaks when you are home, even if just a few moments to sit on your front stoop. Face the sun and, with eyes closed, imagine your heart opening up to the healing solar energy.

✓ If you are close to a beach, try lying on the warm sand without a towel beneath you. This feels even better than a hot stone massage. The sand will blanket one side of your body and refract the sun's energy in each grain. After a few moments, turn over and place the other side of your body on a fresh area of warm sand. Just close your eyes and let the feeling turn your muscles into putty.

Do a Morning Body Scan

In the morning after your alarm goes off (and if you do need to use an alarm, I recommend a gentle one of graduated light or sound), just stay in bed for a few moments with your eyes closed. Do a body scan where you focus awareness on each section of your body and note where you might be holding any sadness or tension. Take a deep breath and direct your breath right to that area, imagining fresh oxygen arriving right to that spot and melting the aches and pains away. Now go to the next area of your body and observe how it feels. If there is tension, repeat this exercise until you are relaxed and loose and ready to gently arise and begin your day. Getting up a half hour earlier will give you the time you need to start your day gently.

Detach from the Hustle and Bustle

One day when I was walking my dog along the shoreline, I looked out into the distance and saw the lighthouse at the end of a rock pier in the next town. A large steamboat had started to float away from the pier and the waters over which it glided gave way to an endless silent calm. The image of this slice of calm, detached from the noise of the mainland, left me awestruck. I thought about the basic human need to purposely withdraw every now and then from the noise of other people's complaints, rude behaviors, criticisms, and rushing around. I imagined myself on that steamship, drifting into oblivion while the noise from the mainland became dimmer and dimmer. Finally silence, just the subtle splashes of the ocean remained. If you visit my website at http://raeleenmaunter .com, you'll find the visualization exercise I now use on a regular basis that was inspired by the insight I got that day at the shore.

Stop to Gaze at Beauty

The "skyscrapers" of Napoli don't come close in height to those of New York. Still, with just thirty-six floors, the Torre Saverio in the *centro direzionale* (administrative center) of Naples takes my breath away with its mirrored beauty. But then, so does an old rural house in Lanola in the Lazio region a little farther north. It was obviously built by hand—not equipment—stone by stone, and like a small castle, it is accented with little wooden arched doors and windows. Even looking at photos of these architectural gems can carry me off to a little piece of paradise when I need it.

My cousin Michele De Filippo's artwork has the same effect on me. Michele's still-life paintings have outlived the artist, but whenever I look at them I see some new small detail: the little brushstroke of cobalt that was previously hiding; the tiny ladybug on the leaf of a flower. My grandfather used to put Michele's paintings on display in the front window of his cobbler's shop. While at first I thought that might have been an odd idea (after all, what do shoes have to do with Italian still-life paintings?), he definitely knew what he was doing. Passersby would stop to stare at the paintings. Then they would smile or marvel to each other. They were mesmerized by the paintings of luscious ripe fruit—baskets of bright yellow bananas, deep burgundy grapes, and spring green pears that curved into the graceful shape of violins. They were uplifted by images of flowers and more flowers—overstuffed vases of calla lilies, baby's breath, and wild poppies that looked as though they'd been freshly picked along the roadside.

Always stop to appreciate the aesthetics around you. Acknowledge how refreshed you feel when you see something you deem as beautiful.

Declare Your Own Personal Sciopero *(Strike) to Do Nothing*

While it may not be politically correct, every now and then I am an advocate of taking a "mental health" day off from work. I know what you are going to say: It's not right, I am not really "sick." That may be true, but protecting your emotional health is just as important as maintaining your physical health. When you are saddened by loss, you need a way to feel like *you* are in control of your recovery and well-being and not dragged around by a routine that will most likely go on with or without you anyway. Be the primary caregiver for yourself. Prescribe yourself a whole day of rest and doing nothing-ness when you most need it.

Say No to Exhausting Tradition

I love good holiday traditions, the kind that energize me and keep me connected with my roots. When you are first going through loss, however, you may not be feeling so festive. You may not have the energy to do all that you have done in years past. It may even be painful to try to keep up the old traditions when you are missing a part of your life that was so important to you.

Lucinda's husband died three months before Mother's Day this year, and, despite her terrible grief, her grown children still expected her to continue on with the festivities. For years Lucinda's husband had really made her Mother's Day special. He made her breakfast in the morning and served it to her with a vase of handpicked wildflowers and a hand-written love note. He went grocery shopping, called the kids, invited them along with their families, and cooked outside on the grill—all to make her day a special celebration.

Lucinda's kids just assumed they were going to her house to celebrate Mother's Day as always. The fact was, Lucinda had very little energy for herself and even less for party making. The last thing she needed or wanted was to cook and clean, and she did not have the courage to ask her children to either invite her out to dinner or have the celebration at one of their homes.

Lucinda reflected on whether or not *she* wanted to celebrate this time around. She finally decided what she really wanted was to retreat from the world for the day and just do nothing. No pressure. No energy drain.

She thought she might end up writing in her journal or just get under the covers and watch old movies. While she knew her children loved her and meant well, she knew she had to declare a *dolce far niente* for the entire day. She felt in her gut that she needed this more than she needed a small crowd around her, even a crowd of her loved ones. She took a deep breath and called her children. To her surprise, each of them understood and respected her need to process what was happening in her life.

Lucinda needed to give herself the gift of a "time-out."

Tips for Enjoying the Sweetness of Doing Nothing

- ✓ Build personal *scioperi* (strikes) into each day.
- ✓ Take a *pisolino* (nap) when you need to.
- ✓ Slow the pace of your rhythm.
- ✓ Do a Lemons into *Limoncello* meditation.
- ✓ Get regular sunlight every day, no matter what the season.
- ✓ Do a morning body scan.
- ✓ Detach from your worries.
- ✓ Stop and gaze at what is beautiful.
- ✓ Say no when you need to.

4

Osservare: Focus on Observations That Heal Your Heart

In rivers, the water that you touch is the last of what has passed
and the first of that which comes; so with present time.

—Leonardo da Vinci

T O CREATE HIS BREATHTAKING MASTERPIECES, Leonardo da Vinci immersed himself in the moment, focusing his attention on details and letting his senses absorb as many stimuli as possible, neither filtering out nor judging what he was observing. *The Notebooks of Leonardo da Vinci* were his effort to record his observations about painting, architecture, mechanics, and the human anatomy. The Renaissance period brought to light the tug-of-war between human reasoning—based on observation—and the traditional dictates of the powerful Catholic Church. The emphasis on objective observation became the basis for what we think of today as scientific thought or empirical observation. Da Vinci's extraordinary capacity to observe detail was evident in his paintings and sculptures, and also in his writings, in which he made reference to *saper vedere*, which means knowing by seeing. Before he would sculpt or paint, Da Vinci observed with refined comprehension. He didn't just look at things casually. He would watch water flow for long periods and note how it moved, the direction it took, how it grooved the rock over which it ran its course, the mist it created, and the change in air temperature as the water fell. He trained himself to notice the detail of every moment. He instructed landscape painters to observe the wind, water, and the setting and rising of the sun in addition to the land itself.

Da Vinci immersed himself in the dynamics of nature and was able to translate his keen observations into awe-inspiring works, which he re-created with masterful hands. No one was more proficient than he in painting the human anatomy, right down to the complexity of the way the skin stretched over the muscle and bones of the human hand or foot. Neuroscientists today still marvel at his textbook accuracy in depicting the human brain. His portrayal of light and shadow on the faces of his portrait subjects made the images he created seem so stirringly real that they could be mistaken for photographs instead of paintings.

Da Vinci's approach in using observation to seek truth shares many similarities with the concept of mindfulness. Staying with a careful observation of the moment, or being mindful of each moment as it comes, allows you to avoid judging, predicting, ruminating, and making yourself miserable by thoughts of either what has already passed or hasn't yet happened. When you are trying to get through a major life challenge, it is tempting to let your fears or thoughts color what is true. There will be times when your mind tells you that you will not be able to survive this. There will be times when you think the world is against you and you will never again have a life worth living. None of those fears correspond to reality. Only nonjudgmental observation, the kind Da Vinci drew from, leads to the truth. The truth is, you can indeed thrive after loss. An entire school of psychology was created to correct subjective self-defeat, the basis from which the late Dr. Albert Ellis developed his rational emotive therapy.[1]

We cannot always trust our thoughts to be rational. For example, we often see the world through erroneous filters. We might habitually block out all that is good with our lives and remain fixated on what we perceive as disastrous. Yes, you have suffered a loss, but what about all of the gifts you still have?

Be Mindful by Focusing on Detail

What would happen if you began to carefully "observe" your life instead of moving through it robotically? My guess is that your courage and inner strength would emerge. You would observe that you have what it takes to survive, and you would begin to appreciate even more deeply how beautiful your life is.

When you engage in focused observation, distressing thoughts begin to melt away. Why? Because you are neither thinking about what has already happened to you nor fearful about what lies ahead. Essentially, when you give yourself permission to do nothing but observe, you are living right in the heart of the moment. Don't put labels on anything; and you will discover what is true. If your puppy is frolicking on the floor at your feet, let yourself laugh and even join in. If a caller says something to upset you, put it out of your mind the minute you hang up the phone, and immerse yourself in the new moment. Past disappointments and future fears are not real; neither one occupies the moment at hand.

Concentration on detail is a great stress reliever. When you lose yourself in the particulars of nature's beauty, your visual cortex is engaged, and you experience peace that can often lead to the sensation of awe. When Abraham Maslow referred to "peak experiences," he was writing about those "awesome" moments that move us in such a way as to create lasting change.[2] Mindfulness can induce these sensations. You can start a mindfulness habit by starting small.

Set aside ten minutes of your day to concentrate only on observing and interacting with what is happening in the moment. If you are washing your car, think about nothing else. Observe the feel of the suds, the warmth of the water. Smell the scent of the detergent, listen to the spray of the hose. Do this for a full ten minutes and you will find that you have a ten-minute vacation from your troubles. Eventually you can start to increase the length of time you spend in mindfulness. You can even break it up into little sessions throughout the day.

Use Mindfulness to Wash Out Painful Memories

Tom and I used to walk down certain neighborhood streets with our dog. In the weeks following Tom's death, however, that same walk was difficult without him. I could have easily avoided those streets, and it would have been fine if I had, at least for a period of time. Instead I chose to practice the kind of mindfulness I had learned from watching my *zia* (aunt) Maria immerse herself fully in whatever she did. I directed my attention to new details of the walk that I had never noticed before. This helped take the focus off the kind of reminders that triggered more grief. Now the walk could become fresh and different, despite its familiarity.

Mindfulness is about being fully present to whatever moment you are living without judging it or rationalizing it. When you live without mindfulness you really rob yourself of your own life. How many times have you heard someone remark, "I wish the springtime would not be over so fast; I hate the heat of summer." Instead of spending that moment enjoying the spring day, the focus is directed toward a dislike for the sweltering days ahead.

The minute you begin to make a judgment about what you are seeing, reality gets clouded. It is true—sometimes the present will elicit sadness. You may come across a reminder of your past that you never wanted to let go. Acknowledge your sadness, then release it and refocus your attention on what you are doing now. This practice will keep you from staying stuck in a cycle of unproductive grief.

Let Yourself Be Awed

Exposure to nature, music, or art that you find inspiring may incite a sense of awe (described as a sense of wonder and expansion), which contributes to a feeling of well-being and tends to make you less attached to material possessions and more connected to your spiritual nature.

The experience of awe gives you the perception of having unlimited time resources. In Italy, time really does seem to go on forever. Many wonderful things unfold in the course of a typical, unhurried day on the boot-shaped peninsula.

When you have been through personal trauma, you realize more than ever how precious time is and how much you don't want your own time to fly by without fully living. Develop your sense of awe by immersing yourself in what you love to do and acknowledging the blessings that offer themselves to you spontaneously. Refuse to rush. Stop frightening yourself and start awing yourself by using the power of your observation.

Mindfulness in Combating Addiction After a Loss

Mindfulness meditation can help break the cycle of addiction. Many of us turn to nonproductive behaviors following loss that can easily turn into addiction. We try to drown out our anxiety with too much food or drink, too many sleeping pills or pain pills. Mindful meditation can actually cause changes to occur in the brain, as evidenced by a comparison of experienced meditators versus novice meditators who underwent functional MRI scans of the brain.[3] Being mindful seems to keep the mind from wandering and may provide relief from anxiety and depression as well as lower blood pressure and strengthen the immune system. Focused attention takes practice and repetition, but it is not hard to do, and well worth the effort.

Make a Mindfulness Minèstra

One of my darkest hours came right after I signed the papers for the sale of my home. In a few days I would be moving out of the house we used to share with our children. I knew I would not be able to maintain it alone. As I looked around the rooms, my mind played back the happy times we shared together: the lively debates we engaged in with our kids, the garden tomatoes and basil that grew each season in the little patch we cultivated, the tree-lined backyard where many a bocce game prompted great camaraderie with extended family members. All of these memories, mostly good but sprinkled with some tough times, too, were part of an average family life acted out on the stage we called home. Now, another ending. I realized that once I turned the key, I would never see the inside of this house again. I was so disturbed by this that I needed to immerse myself in an activity that would calm and reassure me. I decided to make what I call a healthy mindfulness *minèstra* (vegetable soup). I kept my attention focused on each detail of the preparation, and, as I did so, I could temporarily forget my sadness.

From the refrigerator, I pulled out everything that even resembled a vegetable from the produce drawer. There was an eggplant, a sweet potato, one white potato, a bunch of kale, some parsley, fresh basil, a bunch of beets, a large white onion, a head of garlic, and carrots; I found some frozen peas in the freezer, I took out the pot and focused only on the sound of rinsing and then filling the large soup pot half with water then about a third more with some broth I also had in the refrigerator. I put it on the stove and turned the heat up. I kept my attention on task while I was doing this.

I washed and peeled the eggplant, potatoes, and beets and then cubed them with a sharp knife. I sliced the carrots into little orange coins. I listened to the peeling sounds and gazed at the deep aborigine color that revealed a bright white flesh just beneath it. I scrubbed the beets and noticed how they turned the entire cutting board and knife a bright crimson. I smelled the fresh juicy parsley and basil leaves as I chopped them and let their fragrance fill my nostrils. I noticed the irritation in my eyes as I chopped the onion and garlic. Swoosh, everything went into the pot. I turned up the heat, then stood and watched the still water become turbulent and finally transform into a brilliant bubbling boil. I sprinkled in some dried oregano, opened a can of tomato paste and spooned some into the pot, and then I rinsed some dried beans and plopped them into the water like pebbles. Soon, a savory vegetable perfume tickled my nostrils as I stirred the pot. I turned the heat back down to a simmer and walked away from the stove, aware of my own smile. There was no time for self-pity. Time had become another dimension, one that stood still with a very good feeling in my heart. Finally the *minèstra* was ready; I sat down, savored every spoonful very slowly, and, as I did, I envisioned every cell in my body perking up and coming to life.

This single experience gave me the second wind I needed to get through the move. A habit of mindful observation helps us move out of crisis and into a new way of looking at life.

The Italians in my family refused to be restricted by the confines of measured recipes. No one used exact measurements, except when baking, and, even then, creativity could not be denied. Freestyle Italian cooking is the perfect activity during which to practice mindfulness. Just let the process happen without judging or worrying how it will come out. Use whatever ingredients you have on hand and see what you can create while enjoying the process. Remember that the object of this recipe is not only to make a meal but to do it with your full attention to every detail. If you take your time and savor the process, the results will be emotionally and physically restorative. It works for me.

My Mindfulness Minestra

MAKES APPROXIMATELY 8 SERVINGS

Remember, this recipe is meant to be approximate. Think only about the subtask at hand as you do it. Experience each action with all of your senses. For example, what does the pot feel like (heavy, cold, and so on); notice the splashing sound of liquid filling the pot, the sound of vegetables being scrubbed, the shuffle of the beans being rinsed in the colander. Let the aroma of simmering soup fill your kitchen, your nostrils, and your soul.

1 quart filtered water

1 quart of chicken or low-sodium vegetable broth

Assorted root vegetables (beets, potatoes), washed, peeled, and cubed

1 medium onion, diced

4 cloves garlic, minced

1 large eggplant or zucchini, peeled, washed, and cubed

4 large carrots, washed, peeled, and thickly sliced

2 tablespoons tomato paste

½ bag dry beans of your choice (previously soaked overnight) or
1 16-ounce can of beans, rinsed

Assorted fresh or dried Italian herbs (parsley, basil, oregano). If fresh, use a handful of each. If dried, about a tablespoon each.

Sea salt and black pepper (to taste)

2 cups frozen peas

4 cups washed and chopped fresh greens (one of the following or any combination: kale, Swiss chard, collard, or spinach)

Fill a large soup pot two-thirds full with filtered water and broth. Add all the ingredients, except the herbs, salt, pepper, peas, and greens, to the soup pot. Season with the herbs. Add salt and pepper to taste. Stir. Bring everything to a boil, then reduce to a simmer and cover. Cook approximately 45 minutes or until vegetables are tender. Add the peas and greens and let simmer another 10 minutes. Go slow, and enjoy the results.

How to Let Mindful Observation Help You Recover from Personal Crisis

✓ Commit to practicing at least two mindfulness sessions a day, each lasting ten minutes, where you will just *saper vedere*, know by seeing. Do not judge; just notice what you see, feel, and think. Be involved in the actual moments of the experience.

✓ Let awe inspire you and ignite your heart while immersed in the experience. Allow yourself to be enveloped in the beauty of your day, whether you are out in nature, watching an opera on TV, or cooking your own healing minestrone. Observing beautiful sights regularly can bring you moments of wonder.

✓ Breathe. When you wake up in the morning, instead of bounding out of bed, take a few deep slow breaths and notice the feeling of calm that comes over you. Notice how breathing quiets the body and the mind's anxious thoughts. You can do this exercise before you go to bed or even during your lunch hour for a few minutes before or after you eat.

✓ Take a walk in a beautiful park two or three times a week. Make no judgments about what you see; just notice what your eyes are drawn to. What are the colors of nature's gift of life all around you? What are the smells? What is the temperature of the breeze on your skin? Is it misting or drizzling? Notice the coolness against the warmth of your skin. Notice the sounds of the distant airplanes or cars or the chirping of birds or the scampering of squirrels as they search for nuts.

✓ When you are having a conversation, notice more than just the words someone says. Notice their movements, their facial expression, their posture, their vocal tone. Pay attention to every detail. Slow down.

✓ Watch one of your pets. Observe the way your graceful cat grooms herself while basking in the sunlight that comes through the windowpane. Notice how she sits on the ledge with grace and contentment. Watch how she yawns and stretches when she needs to and the sound of her warm purring as you glide a gentle hand over her fur to connect. We can learn a great deal about nurturing ourselves from watching how our pets care for themselves instinctively.

✓ Go to the beach. Follow the distant ship as it floats away into the distance. Feel the warm grains of sand beneath your naked feet as you wiggle your toes. Smell the clean salt air that tickles your nostrils and mists your face as the waves come crashing down in front of you. Note the sound of children's laugher and the splashing of their play as they swim in the blue ocean.

There are so many opportunities to build a mindfulness practice into your life. Notice the relaxing effect mindfulness has on the frazzled emotions caused by loss. You are definitely on your road to healing.

5

Il Regalo: Use the Gift of Your Insight to Make Your Life Better

Chi non ha testa, ha buone gambe.
He/she who has no head, has good legs.
—Old Italian proverb

PHILOSOPHER BENEDETTO CROCE (1866–1952) described the first part of his life as a "bad dream." He was orphaned by the earthquake of Casamicciola in 1883, which left his young life in shambles. The period that followed became a time of going inward, studying, and reflecting about life, which eventually led to his becoming a self-made scholar and one of the most esteemed writers in history. He founded one of Italy's most important literary contributions, *La Critica*, a journal of cultural criticism, believed to lay the foundation for a unified feeling among Italians on the heels of Italy's political

Risorgimento (unification). In a sense, Croce's early tragedy brought out certain gifts that guided him to his personal renaissance.

Stay Grounded and Look for the Insight

Tragedy itself is certainly no gift, but the insight that comes from our crises often is. The quality of the changes brought about as a result of tough times depends on your specific situation, and how you react to it. Many people's lives become more intensely rich and beautiful following personal devastation. We all have the innate ability to be resilient by virtue of the fact that we are human and equipped to handle what may naturally happen to our species. The Italians in my life showed me that personal resilience comes from continually taking simple steps forward. They taught me how to stay involved with all of the mundane events in a day (they keep one grounded), and take inventory of one's blessings like there's no tomorrow. The insights you gain as you come through your loss can lead to a richer quality of life. Avoid all tendencies to filter out some parts of your life in order to dwell on others. It is tempting to focus only on your loss and forget about the parts of your life that are positive and good. Integrating both positive and negative events, however, is how we learn to work in harmony with reality.

We all have to deal with major crises over the course of our lifetimes. The good news is that resilience after personal loss is more common than was originally presumed. One perspective on why this is so comes from the work of researcher George Bonanno. He observed that people who cope well with violent or life-threatening events are usually regarded as heroes, whereas people who cope well with common bereavement following loss are often not mentioned in the literature on resilience; they are frequently dismissed as cold or unfeeling, not resilient. Resilience, as Dr. Bonanno defines it, is the ability to maintain a stable equilibrium while going through the traumatic experience of loss.[1]

Not only does personal resilience lead to a sense of well-being, but positive emotions have a protective effect on our physical health, too. There are many reasons to find ways to "weather our storms" with calm. Translating the insights you gain from your experience into action infuses your life with meaning. Also, you never know when you are inspiring someone else by your example.

Since her childhood days in a little town in Sicily, Claudia had wanted to free women from the long-held tradition of wearing black and other dark colors for years at a time following the death of a spouse or other family member. For as long as she could remember, Claudia's biggest wish had been to own a clothing boutique whose main mission would be to bring color, texture, and renewal to the bereaved.

Her boutique was a kaleidoscopic mix of bright fluorescents, light pastels, and rich gemstone colors that lured passersby inside. For years women would come in feeling depleted and leave looking energized. Not a day went by in which Claudia took this privilege for granted. Then, on the tenth anniversary of the store's opening, Claudia's husband was suddenly killed in a car accident. Not long after that she also lost her store, as Italy's economy took a downturn. Claudia was devastated. She had lost her love, and now, the work she loved.

After taking the time she needed to get her bearings, Claudia had no choice but to take a job at a large department store in Rome to pay her bills. The store manager made her a low-level sales representative and put her in the bedding department, a specialty she had no experience with. She had a rigid time schedule, and, because her coworkers were so much younger than she, she often felt excluded. She had no idea how to use the computerized technology in the store, as she had never used anything like that in her boutique. Claudia began to lose confidence in herself and her ability to go on.

Claudia's mother ultimately motivated Claudia to stay hopeful and turn the pain of her tragedy into a better life. She recounted the story of how their ancestors made it through loss, trauma, and unthinkably impoverished lives in Sicily at the turn of the century. Mamma showed photographs of Claudia's great-grandfather, uncles, and cousins taken during that period and told the story of each one's courage in the face of personal tragedy. These figures in the pictures stood so proud and tall despite weathered faces and tattered clothes. Claudia's mother was telling her daughter about what psychologists call "hardiness."

Researchers have found that a trait called "hardiness" plays an important role in how resilient we are in the face of loss.[2] According to grief researcher George Bonanno, hardiness has three dimensions:

1. Dedicating yourself to finding a meaningful **purpose** to your life
2. Believing that you can **influence** what happens to you
3. Holding a conviction that you can **grow** from both negative and positive life experiences[3]

While most theories describe hardiness as a personality trait, it is also true that personality is just a consistency in our overt and covert behaviors—what we think, feel, and do on a regular basis. Thus you can actually make your personality hardier by practicing behaviors that give your life purpose, as well as seeing your crises as challenges to grow from instead of as threats that will defeat you.

Purpose + Control + Growth = Hardiness

Claudia, in the example above, obviously had to find something that gave her *purpose* again. The question of "Now what?" became the focal point of her *lascia stare* phase (the initial period following loss).

I remember once being asked on a job interview, "What is your personal mission statement?" Although I had heard of companies having mission statements, the idea of an individual figuring out an overarching guiding principle for life was intriguing to me. It didn't take long to answer the question. My personal mission statement is to use my skills, talents, and training to motivate people to live healthy, happy lives.

Because Tom's life was cut short by a heart attack, I decided to work on a cardiac study at Yale teaching stress-reduction techniques to those with heart problems. My general mission statement had not drastically changed, but it became more targeted. Helping people take better care of their hearts gave me a more specialized purpose after my loss.

What is *your* purpose now? How has it changed since your loss?

Here is a straightforward way to clarify your own purpose in the wake of your crisis:

- ✓ Take a journal or notebook and simply write out a mission statement for yourself.
- ✓ Ask yourself questions such as:
  - ✓ Has my mission statement changed since my loss?
  - ✓ How has it changed, or why has it not changed?
  - ✓ How will I fulfill my mission statement in the short and long term?
  - ✓ Where can I use my skills and talents to make positive changes for myself and others?

✓ Revisit your journal for the next couple of weeks, and jot down any additional notes or make modifications.

Influence What Happens in Your Life

Hopelessness—feeling that nothing you can do will change your circumstances—is closely linked to depression, according to researcher Martin Seligman.[4] It may be true that you can't rewind time and take back your past, but you can very much control at least *some* of the things that happen from this day forward. If you make your own breakfast, it is *you* who chooses what foods you eat and how to prepare them. If you dress yourself, it is you and you alone who chooses, from head to toe, the outfit you are wearing. Reminding yourself that there are some things you *do* have control of will help you feel calm and reassured, and less likely to let what you cannot control make you feel like a victim.

Write down a list of all the things you know you have control over right now. You make the choices. Here are some examples:

✓ Whether or not I invite my cousin over for lunch
✓ Whether or not I accept my nephew's wedding invitation
✓ Where I walk my dog
✓ What I will eat for supper
✓ Which CD I will put on the stereo
✓ Whether I go for a walk or not
✓ What I will get at the grocery store

The purpose of this exercise is to make you aware that even though things "happen" to you in life that you cannot do anything about, there are always things that you *can* do something about. This exercise sends a message that the entire world isn't quaking beneath your feet and threatening to swallow you up.

Find Ways to Keep Growing and Evolving

Experience is our teacher. What kind of insight can you get from your experience of loss? Sometimes you know something on an intellectual level, but your loss makes you understand it in an entirely new way. Although I always thought about how short life is here on earth, after Tom's sudden death I never presume that I or anyone else will be around tomorrow. I am more focused on the importance of kindness, generosity of heart, and of not tolerating nonsense from people who want to make me feel miserable. I want to spend my precious moments surrounded by great people and experiences that I can get excited about. Life is a limited commodity and I do not take even one minute for granted.

A year after she lost Umberto—and her store—Claudia's life was once again filled with joy. While initially there were many things that frustrated her about her department-store job, she ended up doing such a great job helping people purchase their bedding and accessories that even the younger employees looked up to her as their expert bedding stylist. Claudia made new friends of all different ages throughout the store, and she began dating a gentleman who worked on a different floor. Although she had to move out of their apartment and find a less expensive rental, she was so proud to be able to pay that rent all on her own. She is learning to trust her own decisions without depending on others' advice and is becoming more self-reliant than ever. Because Claudia is no longer an overworked entrepreneur, she is able to balance her work life more with a social life. The moment she clocks out of the store, she looks forward to having dinner with her girlfriends, or visiting her mother, or going out for a walk with her new beau. Claudia's life is definitely a work in progress. It is a lesson to us all on how to get back to happiness when we feel we've lost everything.

Stories abound of people who changed their lives after a crisis. Maria learned that as independent as she always was, it was okay to seek help for getting through her grief after she lost her daughter to complications of a kidney transplant. Maria has made a list of the friends she knows she can count on when she needs company or a shoulder to cry on, and she encourages herself to make a call the first moment she feels a wave of grief coming on. The woman who Carrie thought was one of her closest friends failed to show up to offer support after Carrie's sister died. Carrie used this as a turning point to make some much-needed changes in the landscape of her relationships. She stopped spending time with people who she identified as "false friends" and began deepening the relationships with people who were loyal friends. After Daria's brother was murdered at the age of forty-two, Daria realized that she could not take even one day of her life for granted. She vowed to never go through her day as if on automatic pilot. She enrolled in a Buddhist meditation class; she has regained her serenity and takes time to notice the joys and pleasures packed into each of her days.

Consider the ways in which your personal crisis has brought about positive change in you:

- ✓ Will you take on volunteer work in the memory of your loved one?
- ✓ Will you enter local politics to work for change in your community?
- ✓ Will you be more tolerant of people who grate on your nerves?
- ✓ Will you start taking better care of your physical and mental health?
- ✓ Will you start making more time for family and friends?

Remind Yourself of Your Gifts and Lessons Each Day

The gift of new insight waits just behind the dark door of grief. If you dare to open that door, you will find the opportunity for personal and spiritual growth that will make you feel much better about living. Whether you decide to practice more self-forgiveness, have more compassion for others, or learn to grasp each *dolce vita* moment that life offers you, allow your life to be changed in a positive and productive way by your loss. If you do, the agony of your loss will not have been in vain.

Using Your Gift of Insight

✓ Stay grounded as you go forward.

✓ Remember the formula: **Purpose + Control + Growth = Hardiness.**

✓ Develop hardiness by reflecting on:

  ✓ Your sense of purpose.

  ✓ The things in your life that you still can control.

  ✓ Turning your loss into personal growth and even a benefit for others.

6

L'arcobaleno: Accept a Rainbow for What It Is

There is no certainty; there is only adventure.

—Dr. Roberto Assagioli, founder of the psychosynthesis movement

EONARDO DA VINCI WASN'T CONSIDERED A GENIUS because of his *Mona Lisa*. Yes, he was a gifted painter, but so were many of his Renaissance-era peers. According to historian J. H. Plumb, what really made Da Vinci a trailblazer was his thirst to understand the true nature of things and not try to make nature into something it is not.[1] Science in that day was based on trying to manipulate nature in an attempt to gain power. To those alchemists Da Vinci said contemptuously, "Go and take your place with the seekers of gold." Da Vinci sought only to appreciate the structure and processes of nature, which were dynamic and ever changing. His passion for appreciating the details of "what is" without trying to change anything would later form the basis of the scientific method of experimentation used today.[2]

Loss uproots us. At first you may deny what has happened, or put it out of your mind. Yet we can only achieve personal growth when we accept the nature of things, and the way life works—the good and the bad—as Da Vinci did. When we try to rewrite nature, we come up empty-handed and more frustrated than ever. Nature is always in the process of change, and, similarly, our circumstances will keep changing throughout our lifetimes. Be assured that bad times and good times are cyclical, as life flows on. You may be at your lowest point now, but that, too, will change. You can see that fact for yourself when you look back on the challenges you have already dealt with over the years.

Acknowledge the Good, Not Just the Bad

A colleague from the University of Parma and I were once on our way to a meeting when he suddenly brought his Alfa to a grinding halt in the middle of the road. With the motor left running, he jumped out his door and hoisted himself up a nearby pole. He did this all just to get a better view—of a rainbow. The urgency of savoring that moment of beauty created a major *ingorgo* (traffic jam), but no one, despite the ensuing *clacson* (chaos), horn-beeping, gesticulations (some obscene)—*really* seemed too put out. There seemed to be an unspoken under-standing among Italians everywhere that a rainbow sighting *certamente* (certainly) takes precedence over getting to a meeting on time. One must stop and enjoy the colors when presented, because soon they will evaporate, as is the nature of the *arcobaleno* (rainbow). But that is okay, too. When the light show has ended, you don't chase after it; you just get on with your day.

When we lose something in our lives that we wanted to keep, it feels like a door was just slammed in our face that we can never again walk through. But by its very nature, life is a continuum of doors closing and opening. It is too easy to generalize our catastrophe. We look for evidence as to why everything else in our life is bad instead of standing back, taking a wider focus, and looking at the more complete picture. Life has good elements and bad, beauty and tragedy, ups and downs. Other doors are opening right now as you read this. Pay attention to them and walk through. We cannot argue with what is. We can only graciously accept what we are given, without becoming so attached to the past that we are unable to function when it evaporates.

Gratitude for what is good in the moment will help us move through the difficulties that we have to face. Being grateful for "what is," without demanding that it change, gets us thinking from a larger perspective. It helps us understand that, although we have lost, we have also had gains, and we will again have both. For an exercise to help broaden your perspective of your life "as it is," visit http://raeleenmautner.com.

If Something Doesn't Go Your Way Despite Your Efforts, Let It Go and Move On

When I was thirteen, my mother unexpectedly gave my dog away. I had waited all of my little life for my parents to give me permission to have a dog. I had begged, pleaded, and insisted, despite all their initial objections. Finally, my mother gave in, although she wasn't too keen on the idea. The day I got the dog was the happiest day of my childhood! I promised I would care for him, walk him, and do everything I could to make him a great member of our family. I even let my mother name the dog, because I could sense she had only agreed reluctantly. I noticed how Mom would keep a distance from Caesar, and when he barked she would seem to panic. Yet I was determined to eventually make this beautiful puppy become her best friend, too.

One day, Mom announced that a man she worked with was going to come in about a half hour and take my dog away and bring it to his home. She reassured me that Caesar would be going to a good home. I was shocked and devastated. I felt betrayed by my own mother, who had never done anything like that before. I remember standing by helplessly as my furry best friend was carried away in the back of this strange man's station wagon, crying for me, and never to be seen again. I was inconsolable for quite a long period of time.

Eventually I learned from my grandmother that my mother had been badly bitten by a dog when she was a child. She was still, after all those years, deathly afraid of dogs, and I came to understand much later on that, although my begging and pleading got her to give into me, it was ultimately disastrous for me to have forced the flow of the natural tide of our family. I knew my mother wasn't enthusiastic about my getting a dog, but I had insisted—a little too much—until I wore her down. She loved me and wanted to give me something that I wanted so much, yet in the end she could not go against her own nature either. I was too young to realize that we should not try to force a door open, even if we can get it to open by force. The truth is, that door may be hard to open because it shouldn't be opened. The day would eventually come when the experience of adopting a dog would be an effortless and happy occasion. Had I had the wisdom I have now, I could have saved us both that turmoil and refocused my attention on other things instead of whining about wanting a dog. As it turned out, having a dog at all costs at that time in my life caused more upset than never having had one.

How to Be Satisfied with Your Life "As Is"

The great Italian psychiatrist Roberto Assagioli, who was a contemporary of Sigmund Freud, founded the psychosynthesis school of psychology. Dr. Assagioli believed that the concepts we expose ourselves to visually produce the reality suggested by the image. In a 1974 interview with *Psychology Today*, Assagioli explained that "images or mental pictures and ideas tend to produce the physical conditions and external acts that correspond to them." With his patients, he used a series of cards meant to trigger desirable attitudes. He believed that words such as *calm, patience, bliss, energy,* and *goodwill* actually summoned up the very quality they represented.[3]

Along the same lines, you can perform this simple exercise at home and begin to transition your emotional state from downhearted to lighthearted. Your focus will be on accepting life on its own terms, knowing you can deal effectively with both good times and bad while all the while appreciating the fleeting nature of a rainbow:

1. Make a list of the ten things you absolutely love about your life right now, *despite your loss*. What are you most grateful for today? Is it your child whom you've loved since the day she was born? The girlfriend who came over with dinner to comfort you? The sun that felt glorious on your skin this morning as it streamed through your window?

2. Write each of the ten gratitude concepts into a sentence. As an example: "I am so happy that I have my daughter in my life." "I am very grateful I have a friend like Julie who brings supper because she cares about me." "I am fortunate to have a chance to feel the sun on my skin as I walk to my office building in the morning."

3. Cut ten large flashcards from cardboard or blank white paper, and transfer each concept to one card.

4. Cut out five more cards. On each one, write words that trigger the feelings you would like to feel right now, for example, *lighthearted, joyful, happy, confident,* or *calm.*

5. Place these flashcards in places where you will see them frequently throughout the day. Read them often until you begin to feel the feelings of the words you are reading. You can add to or subtract these gratitude flashcards according to how well they describe your life in the present.

Enjoy Your Life with Less Attachment

Pain, according to Italian psychoanalyst Roberto Assagioli, forces us to go inward and detach from the illusions of the external world. We have no choice but to look inward for guidance and inner light and eventually become truer to ourselves. Our *attachment* to our earthly situation can actually keep us from fully enjoying the people and possessions in our lives. Dr. Assagioli made a distinction between enjoyment and attachment. He believed that enjoyment was gratuitous and pure. Attachment is "greedy and expectant." Attachment, explained Dr. Assagioli, is past or future centered. It is about wanting something we had before that we don't have now, or worrying that we will not have it again.[4]

Enjoyment is about reaping pleasure from this moment. This is where we need to stay. It is important to see the larger picture and to take note of all the things you can enjoy right now, without giving any one thing too much importance. Assagioli believed that there are endless possibilities for experiencing enjoyment. When we get too attached to something (food, for example), we become gluttonous. We begin to crave food, instead of putting it in its proper place—taking the right proportion and then moving on to something else. Nonattachment takes practice, as many of us get our security from holding on. When we accept the transient nature of life, we can continually discover the new enjoyment in any given moment. We begin to realize that joy is not just a thing of the past.

Brenda was on cloud nine when she fell in love with Edward, a man she met in her adult education class. Life was starting to feel good again. That was, until she came down with the flu and had to stay in bed for two weeks. Edward, a self-proclaimed outdoors person, admitted he wasn't the type to stay indoors playing Florence Nightingale. Brenda was hurt initially but thought once she got better, Edward would certainly show up again at her door to apologize. Instead, she got an e-mail letting her know he had found someone else. Brenda had learned to accept events as they unfolded. She turned her focus to other things that made her happy and distracted her from dwelling on Edward. She felt that she was meant to take a different direction, because, if Edward had really loved her, he certainly would not have turned out to be so uncaring. Brenda began to spend more time having fun with her girlfriends and babysitting her little granddaughter. She made a deliberate effort to write out flashcards to remind her to feel *happy, loving life,* and *emotionally strong.* She looked at those images each day, and she felt herself becoming the words on the cards.

Learn the Rainbow's Lesson

While we shouldn't go chasing rainbows, it is imperative to enjoy the rainbow when it does appear. When it inevitably slips away, though, we must "let go" of our need to have it remain in the sky forever and go against its own nature. We must stop worrying about whether or not we will ever see another one. This way of thinking takes practice but it is the ticket to serenity. Keep in mind that everyone and everything on earth is just passing through. The same applies to you. Know that you will continue to get called upon to let go of what you love. Do this with dignity and inner peace. You will also be given new experiences to love. Open your heart, and love them, too.

Create Multiple Experiences of Pleasure

Life is worth living when you are able to fully enjoy it. Find ways to create lots of pleasure-filled experiences every day. Pleasure is good for the heart, mind, body, and soul. Here are some ideas to start with:

✓ Send an e-mail to as many people you like as possible. Invite them to a potluck supper at your home. Everyone brings a dish, and you do nothing more than wait to see who shows up. You will have a great time with very little effort.

✓ Clarify what your passion is and research how to follow that passion more fully; for example, if you have always wanted to be a yoga teacher, then do some research to see what the training involves. Send out inquiries to local yoga instructors and ask them for their advice on how to get started.

✓ Buy new clothes, get a new hairdo, or purchase new shoes in a style you are not used to wearing. Break out of the old mold and discover a new you inside.

✓ Volunteer to read to the blind, or do crafts with sick children in the hospital. You will get a terrific feeling from doing something that makes a real difference in others' lives.

✓ Go to a new museum and linger over the paintings that attract you. Just enjoy the sensation of being inspired, without overthinking or trying to interpret what the artist meant.

✓ Start trusting—and following—your intuition. What do you feel like eating for supper tonight? Do you feel like going to a movie after dinner or going for a walk? Give yourself options and then be directed by your bliss. Watch how your life blossoms.

You will feel better when you practice accepting nature on its own terms. Don't go against the nature of things or try to impose your will on the natural course of events. Beware when you find yourself expending a lot of effort in trying to attain a certain outcome that won't happen. Go instead where life takes you and trust in your ability to handle whatever comes your way.

Accepting Life's Rainbows

✓ Learn to accept the changing nature of life's experiences.

✓ Acknowledge the good in your life, even when you are going through tough times.

✓ Be satisfied with your life "as is."

✓ Post flashcards of gratitude throughout your home where you will see them often.

✓ Begin to live with less attachment.

✓ Find ways to enjoy something about each and every day.

Pian Piano:
Go Slowly but Surely

7

La Bellezza: The Power of Beauty to Lift Your Spirits

A beautiful thing never gives so much pain as
does failing to hear and see it.

—Michelangelo

IT WAS A RAINY DAY IN ROME when I ducked into a coffee bar to avoid getting soaked. Too late I noticed an elderly woman right behind me just as I let the door close behind me. I quickly reopened the door, held it open for her, and smiled.

"*Mi scusi, signora,*" I said. "Excuse me."

"Oh," she remarked, "what a beautiful yellow scarf you have on. It makes it seem like the sun is out, even in this rain."

"Thank you," I said.

"*No no, grazie a lei,*" remarked the woman. "Thank YOU."

One of the tenets of psychosynthesis psychology, founded by Roberto Assagioli, is that crisis can serve as the beginning of a new journey of self-exploration.[1] Infusing your senses with beauty—a beautiful sight, a pleasing sound, smell, thought, or experience—can renew your conviction to carry on. Daily doses of beauty can hasten your emotional recovery following loss. Transpersonal psychologist and bestselling author of *La Bellezza e L'anima* (*Beauty and the Soul*) Piero Ferrucci claims that beauty is not an "extra"; rather, it is essential because it has the power to change our lives. As one example, he describes the reaction of legendary dancer Isadora Duncan, who told how she sat for hours before Botticelli's famous *Primavera:*

> I sat there until I actually saw the flowers growing, the naked feet dangling, the bodies swaying; until the messenger of joy came to me and I thought, "I will dance this picture and give to them this message of love, spring, procreation of life which had been given to me with such anguish. I will give to them, through the dance, such ecstasy."[2]

You can tell by this passage the powerful and positive effect that visual beauty—such as that found in the arts—can have on a person's emotions. According to Ferrucci's research, beauty is so powerful that it can give people back their love for life, heal emotional wounds, make worries seem lighter, and help us gain more mental clarity.[3] Furthermore, when recovering hospital patients were exposed to visual beauty, it also appeared to ease physical suffering.[4]

The idea of beautifying hospitals with artwork is nothing new. In 1419 Brunelleschi sculpted the façade of a foundling hospital in Florence, and pre-Renaissance sculptor Nicola Pisano created statues that would eventually comfort the sick in hospitals. But in modern times, researchers began to wonder how effective beauty is in helping people to recover from their ailments. Researchers from Bari, Italy, found that when we look at beautiful artwork, our pain level decreases. Beautiful art can be both distracting and healing, and increasingly more medical centers and hospitals are paying attention to the aesthetics of their interior design as a way to create an ambience of beauty for people with chronic pain. Could pleasant surroundings lessen the impact of one's sensation of pain? It was found that the distractive effect, together with how pleasing the artwork is to the person viewing it, actually could help a person feel less pain. The results emphasized the cognitive basis of aesthetic perception, how subjective pleasure, when it comes to experiencing art for example, can moderate pain perception and may even improve health.[5]

One English study found that patients had a 21 percent shorter recovery time when their hospital space was designed to be a beautiful dwelling of light, color, and exquisite furniture design and blocked out unpleasant noise. Patients also seemed to feel less anxious, complained less, and had less need for painkillers, according to Ferrucci.[6]

Recovering from personal loss is really an integrative journey, one that requires you to take special care of your body, your spirituality, your emotions, and your mind. People often undervalue the importance of beauty. Instead they think first of utility, "Why bother planting flowers if we could grow something to eat in that space?" While beauty may not address a functional need, it is absolutely a necessary nutrient for healing and well-being.

Studies show that people who expose themselves regularly to the experiences that *they* perceive as beautiful—whether by going to museums or the theater, gazing at natural landscapes, attending an exquisite concert, or even placing favorite flowers and pictures around their homes—can make them feel happier to be alive and even increase their longevity.

Some people dismiss the value of beauty because it is free. In our get-what-you-pay-for culture, beauty for its own sake is devalued as a waste of time. Is it a waste of time to avail yourself of something that will lift your mood, clear your mind, and may even strengthen your immune system? On the contrary, surrounding yourself with beauty following loss should be valued as one of the *best* uses of your time and effort. In this phase of *pian piano* (slowly, slowly), start slowly to move ahead, and you need only take little steps that will put you square into the experience of beauty. Aesthetic beauty is revered in the Italian culture and has been since the beginning of time. It is part of what constitutes those little *piccole-grandi cose* (small but great things) that make Italians so content with everyday life.

Keeping your surroundings beautiful will make you feel like smiling again. It can help you feel happier, cared for, and give you clarity of mind while you take the time you need to process your loss, sort out your emotions, thoughts, and those feelings that bubble up around a major life change.

Humankind's thirst for beauty is not new. Historian J. H. Plumb described the Renaissance era as the pursuit of beauty "as if it were a drug."[7] Everyone wanted to adorn their abodes, the places they frequented, even themselves in sunlight gold, silver, bronze, silks, rubies, and emeralds. A quest for beauty was the common denominator. Beauty made people feel good. It elevated the soul. It brought craftsmanship in painting and architecture to new heights of appreciation. The dawn of oil painting technique lent itself to more creative uses of light and shadow, which made everything seem more real and detailed. Even the human expression of suffering, which found its way into artistic masterpieces, emanated a sorrowful beauty through its confirmation of unity among us all.

To Michelangelo Buonarroti, who grew up in Florence during the high Renaissance to become one of the most acclaimed artistic geniuses in the history of the world, beauty was sacred. Beauty was how God communicated to man, and thus Michelangelo portrayed the exquisite beauty of the human body—with all of its details, curves, and musculature. His famous sculptures *Pietà* and *David* can awe you as deeply as his frescoes on the ceiling of the Sistine Chapel. All beauty, it was believed at the time, came from God. This belief in the sacredness of visible beauty served as a testimony to how it can transform us. A simple yet powerful moment can be experienced when we pause to drink in the colors of a painting, the graceful lines of a sculpture, the delicateness of a field of wildflowers.

Visual art does not have to be "happy," in the traditional sense of the word, to be healing. It just has to be beautiful in some way, to the one who beholds it. Sometimes the emotional solidarity of a sad painting can ease your burden, just as talking about your troubles with a good friend can lighten the load. In an article entitled "Art and the Mind," Noel Carroll discusses how art can allow us to explore a mood and reflect on it.[8] This can be beneficial when trying to come to terms with loss. Sometimes a cheery painting is not what you need. Your soul instead seeks its match, and from that feeling of solidarity you begin to feel relief.

Aesthetic beauty speaks a universal language that teaches us about the nature of the human condition. In fact, the *chiaroscuro* technique that is most often associated with Leonardo da Vinci was about making the imagery in paintings much more realistic. This gave way to depicting everyday life with extraordinarily realistic lighting. Scenes of commonplace events such as ordinary conversations and common card games as well as traditional biblical scenes of the Madonna and the saints then became even more relatable.

Michelangelo Buonarotti's *The Creation* (painted around 1508–1512) is a fresco adorning the ceiling of the Sistine Chapel in the Vatican in Rome. The famous image of a white-robed God the Father surrounded by angels is interpreted by Italian researchers Tranquilli, Luccarini, and Emanuelli as a "placenta" that reaches out to and almost touches a younger, naked image of himself, that of Adam.[9] Adam's hand is rather limp and appears to be from the separate, more grounded earth where he looks up wistfully at God, who appears to be floating away with the heavenly spirits surrounding him. The concept of letting go in this piece reminds us that the Almighty is never far, even though at times we feel we are alone. This painting, in its lifelike simplicity, is to me representative of the grace and strength of the human spirit.

In an address delivered at the Minnesota Medical Association in 2011, Professor Robert Veninga said that "resilience is baked into the heart of the universe."[10] We all live with temporary conditions. Life does not have to be about letting the despair of loss immobilize us. The question is, how do we remain upbeat and continue on with our lives when we are facing difficulty and challenge? "First," said Veninga, "the soul needs play time."[11] At our deepest level of being, we need to unplug and just refocus. Exposing ourselves to various experiences of beauty—for beauty's sake alone—is one way to clear our thoughts of the day-to-day *trantràn* (routine), and, like smelling salts when one is faint, aesthetic beauty revives us.

The Power of Beauty

Campodimele, a mountaintop Italian village surrounded by fields of wildflowers and beautiful nature and whose name means field of honey, is renowned for its reputation as the village of longevity. The high likelihood that people will live well into their nineties has most often been attributed to hard work, sound sleep, and, above all, a fresh and healthful diet. I would add something else to the mix: There is inherent beauty in the rhythm of the residents' lifestyle. One business owner from that town told me that the people of this remote little town get up at sunrise, work with the land all day, and go to bed at sunset—almost without exception. They are self-sustaining and don't let the "noise" of the cities outside their walls penetrate their well-being and stress them out.

Beauty can be found in a simple, stress-free, noise-free life. For me, beauty is quietude. I love the calming sounds of a forest, the meditative atmosphere of a church or museum, or even in a little out-of-the-way antique shop where the store owner, who is the only person there, starts letting me in on the "secrets" of the beautiful objects from long ago. Beauty, all of it.

At Yale, I taught cardiac study participants to visualize the most beautiful scene they could imagine. This technique brought them inner peace and a sense of joy, as evidenced by their comments to me. This form of deep relaxation lowers the level of stress hormones that put the heart at risk for arrhythmia. A beautiful scene can induce peace, feelings of relaxation, harmony, and well-being.

When I was growing up, there was a print on a wall at my grandmother's house of two beautiful young women in long graceful gowns— one of mint green, the other of wheat gold. The woman in green was seated before the harp, her graceful fingers just about to create music. The other woman stood behind her; she may have been the music teacher waiting for her student to perform. When I was troubled about something, I would sit in front of that image and lose myself in the fantasy—I would become one of those women in the flowing ball gowns about to make sweet angelic music, all tranquil and content. My grandmother's home was small, but she had modest objects of beauty positioned everywhere the eye might come to rest. A deep amethyst-colored cordial glass and decanter set from her native Sicily formed the center visual in her curio cabinet. Two ornate German steins her son brought home from his military duty stood proudly on her bookcase alongside oval photos in swirly gold frames of her mother, father, and grandparents. Despite those special treasures, her home was not cluttered. Airy spaces, to her, were beautiful. They kept the mind free. On the periphery of her home was the Sicilian flower garden that gave us color shows each season: bursts of vibrant oranges, purples, blues, and pinks smattered about. Each day when I came home from school, I would stand for a few moments in front of the garden and be cheered by its sweet perfume.

Find Ways to Put More Healing Beauty into Your Life

When you lose something or someone important to your life, it is doubly important to take time each day to engage in beauty rituals that will help your heart lighten up. Here are some ideas:

✓ Buy some inexpensive prints of paintings you love. Frame them and place them in key areas of your home, like right where you come in the front door.

✓ Rent a film that inspires you. Some of my favorites and high on the scale of moving beauty are *La Vita è Bella (Life Is Beautiful)*, *Ciao, Professore,* and *Benvenuti al Sud (Welcome to the South)*. The story lines are about people who are positively transformed by their experiences. You can rent these or other movies with beautiful story lines.

✓ Notice beauty around you each day. Take delight in the little round face of a baby, a field of rolling green grass, or the panorama of a busy city from the stillness of a hillside.

✓ Go to out-of-the-way, unique little artisan shops. Admire the objects of beauty that someone put their heart and soul into.

When your eyes send messages of beauty to the brain, your stress hormones decrease, your mood lightens, and you remember that life is good despite the pain of loss.

Find Beauty Even in Tragedy

In the film *La Vita è Bella,* Italian actor Roberto Benigni showed us that there is beauty in even the most tragic circumstances. That film, set during World War II, depicts a Jewish Italian who was put on a train with his young son. The destination was a concentration camp. His non-Jewish wife insisted that she be on the train with her family, and thus the three went off to a place where unimaginable human suffering was the norm. Guido, played by Benigni, creatively invented a game to help his son survive. In the end, it was Guido himself who was shot when he went out to look for his wife. The story line was remarkable for its human portrayal of the beauty that came from tragedy: the invincible love of a family and the idea that even in the direst of circumstances there is beauty and victory in the courage of the human spirit.

Take Comfort in Beautiful Art

The visual arts of the Italian Renaissance draw their healing power from universally recognized depictions of life. The interactions depicted in various scenes have human and spiritual themes that cut across time and geography. Familiarity comforts. That may be why the Madonna and child image is compelling to so many. Motherhood is a recognizable and comforting human and spiritual archetype. When we go through a frightening transition, we want to revert to what comforted us as children. We want to feel small again and protected by mother's loving arms. You can get that feeling by immersing yourself in beautiful classic art. Like a soothing balm for a wounded heart, Sandro Botticelli's *Madonna della Loggia* can provide the comforting feeling of nurturing, the spiritual uplift of visual beauty, and the image of hope, reassurance, and most of all, love. You get a feeling of reassurance as you look at the chubby little figure staring intensely into his mother's face as the Madonna presses her head to her child's forehead; her expression is serene as she gracefully supports his body with her gentle hands. Five minutes of absorbing this beautiful image can really turn your mood around.

Make Your Home More Beautiful

An Italian home can run the gamut, from homey simplicity to high-tech design. The modern designs of Raffaello Pravato (of the famous Italian kitchen design company Scavolini) express his vision of blending the elegance of classic materials like fine wood and stone with the contemporary feel of steel and glass. This satisfies the preferences of those who like both the feeling of old classics with the contemporary feel of modernity. Your home, too, should reflect what you think is beautiful. No matter how you decide to style and arrange the inside of your home—whether minimalist or ornate or something in between—it should reflect warmth, pleasantness, and security that pleases *you.* It is not about buying expensive draperies or break-the-bank furniture. The real beauty of a home lies in its ability to make you feel great, much like the experience we get from looking at a beautiful painting or a familiar face we love. Don't take this for granted. Let your home be welcoming and uplifting.

Giorgetto Giugiaro is a renowned Italian designer of everything from cars to cameras to pasta shapes. His son Fabrizio refers to him as a "genius" who always believes in proportion, balance, and good quality, but also believes that good taste is an individual thing.[12] The simplicity of a bare-bones kitchen, for instance, invites clarity and a sense of spaciousness. The emphasis should be on functionality of equipment and space enough to move around to prepare the food that nurtures and heals your body. Just make sure that your living spaces both reflect a unique expression of you and make you feel good when spending time at home.

Keep Some—But Not All—Reminders of the Past

There is no time line for adorning your home with more beauty. It is important to take your time and pay attention to what gives you a good feeling. I know some widows who keep their homes exactly as they did when their spouse was alive. A museum-like tribute to the deceased can come at a high price if it keeps you from enjoying your life now.

You can imagine the mementos I had accumulated by the time I lost Tom. My home was filled with photos and artifacts, not to mention his personal belongings—from his bicycle to the old-fashioned camera that he loved to take black-and-white slides with. Getting through my loss required a balance between the beauty of my "old life," which I still needed to give me continuity, and a few signs of the new phase of life I was about to enter. When you face a loss—whether it is the loss of a loved one, a relationship, your health, your property, or a job—the decision of what to remove and what to keep from the past is a very individual thing. My guideline was simply this: I would keep a few objects that reminded me of the life Tom and I shared, then acquire a few new things to balance the constant reminder of death with that of rebirth. I did not want to look around me and have everything make me cry. A few familiar pieces would comfort me when I looked at them, but I blended those "classics" with the "contemporary," to encourage me on to my new life ahead.

Lift Your Spirits with Beauty

✓ Figure out what is beautiful to you.

✓ Expose yourself to beautiful art.

✓ Watch movies whose stories inspire you.

✓ Beautify your home and surroundings.

✓ Keep some beautiful things from your past, but introduce new ones that symbolize your new life ahead.

8

La Semplicità: Simplify for Clarity and Peace

Whether it is a dispersion, or a resolution into atoms,
or annihilation, it is either extinction or change.

—Marco Aurelio

ROMAN EMPEROR AND PHILOSOPHER Marco Aurelio believed it was important to get rid of excess *things*. He wrote:

> Throwing away then all things, hold to these only which are few, and besides bear in mind that every man lives only in this present time, which is an indivisible point, and that all the rest of his life is either past or it is uncertain.[1]

Material clutter creates mental confusion. We can more easily bear what we must when we have mental clarity. In reality, all we really need is what serves us in the present moment. Yet, sometimes our emotional attachment to "things" makes it difficult to let go and simplify our lives.

Material things are not the only things we need to trim from our lives following a major transition. Getting rid of mental clutter, such as excessive disturbing thoughts, is just as important as getting rid of the possessions you don't need. The thought process amongst my Italian family members varies according to the individual, but negative thought rumination is something I have never witnessed among any of them. Both joy and sorrow bring a very real human reaction, but there is no dwelling in either, just a full immersion in the experience of now.

Overscheduling activities can also lead to mental clutter, as well as physical exhaustion. Crossing out some of the activities you have jam-packed into your schedule is part of simplifying, as is eliminating the negative relationships you have kept in your life only because you wanted to avoid making waves. The time has come to take decisive action to make your life simpler. You can do so in small increments or in one fell swoop as I did.

Semplicità (simplicity) is the unspoken law of the land in everyday Italian life. Despite exposure to foreign cultural influences, Italy has managed to hang on to its reverence for *semplicità*. Simplicity does not mean lack of progress, quite the opposite. Uncomplicated living just eliminates the "white noise" in your life so you can focus on what counts now with much less effort and make progress toward your personal renewal. The principle of *semplicità* should become your mantra when you are moving forward from personal crisis. You will feel the load begin to lighten as you unburden yourself of all excess.

Simplify Your Possessions

The preference in Italy is for fewer things of quality as opposed to a plethora of items for accumulation's sake. You would be hard-pressed to find Italians buying duplicates, triplicates, or quadruplicates of items just because they don't know if they already have one somewhere. You don't have to be a pack rat to be living with clutter, either. Clutter comes in degrees. For instance, do you really need four white blouses when you can only wear one at a time? You pay an emotional price for excess that goes far beyond wasting money. The real meaning of your life is not about "things." Let them fall away and show the real you, unobscured by the chaos of your possessions. Make proactive changes today that will let you live more simply and think more simply so that you will have the resources you need to reinvent a life that better reflects who you are on the inside. The act of paring down brings out a more authentic you.

When my realtor called to tell me he had a buyer for my home, I felt like I was falling off a skyscraper in slow motion. I was about to give up the home that Tom and I shared with our children, along with the things that represented our family memories. I knew there was no way I'd be able to take them with me. Almost everything but a few exceptional pieces would have to go. I began to plow through this task, take stock of what I had in each room until everything I designated as extraneous was donated, given away, or trashed. I believe that there are times when we have to trudge through such emotionally charged tasks if we want to begin the healing process. Simplifying your surroundings takes courage and conviction. You have both of these qualities, too.

Simplify Your Thoughts

My dear friend Salvatore once told me that in his opinion, Americans think too much. "We Italians live to emote, while Americans seem like they live to think. Perhaps more of a balance is needed, for if you start to think *too* much, the *dolce vita* is over."

Salvatore was not entirely off base. Negative thoughts regenerate like cancer cells in time of crisis. It is easy to ruminate on our troubles. Cognitive psychologists believe we should challenge disturbing thoughts by asking ourselves if there is any real evidence to justify them.[2] This is generally very effective advice, but when recovering from trauma, we don't always have the emotional resources or the presence of mind to apply this technique. For now, simply clearing your mind of persistent thoughts of anxiety, worry, anger, and sadness will bring you peace. A great way to do this is by taking a few deep, slow breaths (inhale-hold-exhale, all to a slow count of four) whenever you notice your thoughts are making you feel bad.

You are now learning skills and turning them into habits to make your life better. Perhaps something as fundamental as how to set up online banking to pay your bills will make your life easier. Maybe you need to learn how to trust your own instinct, and be more decisive when making choices. Eliminate negative thoughts that don't support you, and substitute them with thoughts that empower you to take action.

Have Simple Fun

The game was called "Which Hand?" ("*Quale Mano?*") Although Nonno Domenico didn't invent the game, he sure delighted us with it when we were children. There were no televisions, video games, fancy board games, headphones, or flashing sights and sounds. The only props Nonno used were his hands and a *noce* (walnut). Inside one of Domenico's broad and callused hands that were permanently darkened by the shoe polish of a *calzolaio* (shoemaker) would be a *noce* that my sister or I would have to locate. He would put his hands behind his back, switch the nut around, and bring his closed fists forward again, and with a devilish grin ask, "*Quale mano?*" "That one! No, that one!" Inevitably I would discover that the hand I chose was empty, but the delirium of engaging in this simple joy made me forget the world around me, no matter what else was happening in my life at the time.

Nonno Domenico's entire life was based on *semplicità* and a respect for balanced living. The way out of grief is to know it is okay to smile and have fun again. Go on and enjoy a few moments of carefree laughter. You deserve to feel lighthearted again and have no reason to feel guilty. Watch that silly cartoon on YouTube or rent reruns of that hilarious old comedy that used to be on TV. Get on the floor and play with your dog. Go for a hike with your friends and have a rollicking good time. You don't need fancy trips or fancy restaurants to make you smile. Just give yourself permission to lighten up with simple fun.

Meditation and Mindfulness

Yale neuroscientist Judson Brewer's research on meditation using functional magnetic resonance imaging (fMRI) of the brain found that when our minds are racing, we experience distress. His work centers on meditation to help calm the mind and on mindfulness to keep it from wandering frantically.[3] While most of us think meditation requires long stretches of time, even consistently setting aside five or ten minutes each day to quiet the mind can bring clarity and inner peace. You can also simplify your mental life through waking mindfulness. Try making a routine of noticing everything you experience. Go outside, for example, when the sun is setting, and focus your awareness on every detail: the shape of the clouds, where the glow of the sun hits the objects it touches, the colors of the sky. Don't judge what you see, just notice the subtleties that you don't usually notice as you go through your day.

Ten Ways to Simplify Your Life

What makes Italian food and wines so exquisite is their simplicity. Italian vineyard owner and wine importer Julius Angelini, in an interview in which he "raised a glass to simplicity," said: "Wine is very simple in its essence: the less grapes (on the vine), the better the wine."[4] The same is true of our lives in general. What are you holding on to that is adding heaviness to your progress? The principle of *semplicità* will help you make room for your new life. A Roman friend once suggested that I select two or three treasures from each of the boxes of photos and documents I had collected over the years. The rest would have to go. I proceeded to adopt this philosophy to pare down every area of my life. It worked wonders. I began to feel freer and more confident about my ability to make other decisions to get my life back on track.

Here are ten suggestions to simplify, Italian-style:

1. **Relationships:** Loved ones are treasured in Italy. There are only two decisions Italians choose from when it comes to others, and it is a good rule of thumb for you to keep in mind if you want to simplify your life:

In or out. When a relationship makes you feel good, keep it. If it makes you feel lousy, weed it out. A person either deserves to be in your circle or not. Do not keep people there who bring you down or don't value you. You know who they are. Draw personal boundaries and eliminate excess noise from your social life. The one exception to this, although not in all cases, is family. We don't choose our family members, yet dealing successfully with challenging family members can teach us what we need to learn about dealing with difficult times.

2. **Simplify Eating:** I hear many people say they don't have time to cook. Well cooking is therapeutic; kitchen slavery is not. People get the impression that they have to spend hours in the kitchen prepping, cooking, and cleaning up afterward. Just the thought of it makes one want to head for the nearest fast food joint, which can add health problems to an already compromised state. In Italy, eating has two straightforward objectives: to nourish the body, and to draw loved ones around the table. There are really no fancy cooking techniques, exotic ingredients, or endless hours of commitment in everyday Italian cuisine. Simply stock your pantry with a few basics and stick to uncomplicated, healthy Mediterranean dishes for now. No complications when it comes to eating. Think healthy and simple. That's all. A bit of arugula, a slice of fresh mozzarella, a few cherry tomatoes, and a drizzle of balsamic vinegar will combine into a lunch fit for an exquisite human being—YOU. If you'd like some starter recipes, just visit my *Lemons into Limoncello* fan page on Facebook.

3. **Vacations:** Vacations are imperative to Italians. They serve as a necessary break from routine and a way to recharge. In these economic times, however, Italians—who usually prefer to vacation in their own country anyway—have found ways to cut expenses even for domestic

vacations.[5] Renting camping spots for less time, going to a less extrava-gant hotel, and deciding to put towels down instead of renting beach chairs—are all ways in which the Italian *arte d'arrangiarsi* (the art of getting by) helps Italy's people take on their challenges with grace and aplomb, while refusing to do without the break from routine, which everyone needs. You don't have to make big, expensive plans for vaca-tion, but you should take at least a simple getaway to distance yourself for a few days from the crisis you have been dealing with. Go somewhere inexpensive—and pull the plug on technology. Sometimes I relish get-ting away for even a day by taking a long drive to a new place. I might bring a little *panino* (sandwich) with me and if the weather is nice I'll find a quaint picnic spot, soak in the beauty of nature, then drive back home. If it is raining I might just sit and watch the weather do its thing from the coziness of my car. When I return I feel refreshed, without any of the chaos or expense of a longer, more formal vacation.

4. **Holidays:** There is a family not far from where I live that celebrates the Christmas season by putting at least fifty inflated figures on their lawn. It takes this family weeks to get all the figures out of the shed, pump them up, anchor them down, put up the lighting, then take them down again, only to start all over again for the next holiday. There is nothing wrong with this, if it is what you like to do. For me, decorations are more beautiful when they are simple and few. Simplicity also creates space for remembering what the holidays are really about. Most Italians still prefer to keep Christmas holy and limit their festivals to church processions, *presepi* (Nativity) Christmas crèches, solemn masses, and breaking bread together. *Semplicità* fosters joy.

5. **Home:** Go through each room and each drawer in each room and each shelf in each room. Eliminate everything you don't use, and make a

mental note to yourself that you will not buy anything else from now on unless you really need it.

6. **Work:** A recent article in the *Corriere della Sera* advised that when at work we should not leave our e-mail open. It distracts us, obscures what we really need to do, leads to wasting time, and brings confusion and stress.[6] Trying to multitask when you've just suffered a loss is not a good idea. Concentrating on one assignment at a time will keep you from feeling distracted and overwhelmed. Give yourself permission to take your time and slow down.

7. **Your Emotions:** Don't let the tensions of the day get to you. Take a moment to chill out after work, focus on the good, and let go of negativity. My friend Vito used to come home and bring his stress through the front door with him. Now, after work he stops at a favorite little greenery area off the Autostrada del Sole, a well-known highway that connects Milan with Naples. It is not a famous Italian tourist spot, but rather a simple stop where you can sit under a tree with a picnic lunch and have a few moments of peace. He brings a little roll filled with a slice of prosciutto and cheese and takes the blanket out of his trunk to lie on the grass. He eats his snack, watches the wildlife play tag around the tree trunks, then packs up and goes home a happy man, which makes his family happier, too.

8. **Your Car:** It isn't logical to think that our car runs better when it's clean, but most of us do feel better driving an uncluttered, clean-smelling car. I start to feel anxious when my car starts to get messy. You don't need to feel like you are riding in a roving landfill in this delicate period of your life. It will zap your energy. This doesn't mean you have to lug out the hose and wash the car by hand if you don't want to. I go to a very inexpensive car wash and then get a damp cloth and wipe out the inside and

shake out the mats. Unclutter the space that surrounds you. You deserve the beauty that comes with organized surroundings.

9. **Your Daily Routine:** Italian daily life unfolds in a slow, reassuring rhythm. Most Italians rise at the same hour, eat at the same intervals, frequent the same coffee bars and stores. Sound boring? Maybe. But for now, you, too, should stay away from drama at all costs. You need the soothing quality of simple routine, however unexciting that might sound. Doing certain things routinely makes them become automatic, requiring less effort on your part and that means more energy for you.

10. **Shopping:** Mom and Pop stores used to be the only choice in traditional Italy. You would walk into a small space and the owner would personally assist you and point out the perfect scarf or sweater. You weren't thrown into an arcade of endless racks under blaring fluorescent spotlights and music that must have been purposely written to raise the blood pressure. There is only one way to deal with shopping: Go in knowing what you want to purchase, go right to those items, buy them, and get out. When you are dealing with loss, it is normal to be more forgetful and distracted than usual. Shopping—whether for clothing, groceries, or even last minute necessities—can be exhausting. Make it easy on yourself: Seek out smaller stores, and go with a list. Shopping online can also be a more serene alternative.

Italian culture is known for its simple traditions. Religious rituals are celebrated to give hope and wipe out loneliness. Breaking bread with friends and neighbors makes a simple glass of homemade wine a celebration. A *passeggiata* (leisurely stroll) creates a simple, enjoyable evening. Simplicity is what makes space for true joy and daily pleasures. Simplicity unburdens the already weighed-down heart and gives it hope and wings. As you reread the ten tips for simplicity, try to come up with additional ways to simplify your life. Let *semplicità* be a gift of peace and lightness to yourself.

Here is one way I personally enjoy simplicity—and great tasting nutrition—in the kitchen (no surprise here!). Nonna D'Agostino would always just take a little of this and a bit of that, throw them together in a big pot, and culinary magic was the result. Learn to cook creatively— not rigidly. Experiment with ingredients you have on hand, and free yourself from complicated recipes. *Pasta e Ceci*—elbow macaroni and garbanzo beans—was one of my favorites, and smelled so good when I walked into Nonna's kitchen. The ingredients I list are approximate, for just as Angelina varied what she put into her dishes, so do I. Here, however, are the basics.

Angelina's Recipe for Simple Pasta e Ceci

MAKES 6–8 SERVINGS

Pasta:

18 cups water (enough to fill a large pot ¾ full)

2 tablespoons salt

12 ounces (about ¾ box) uncooked pasta (small shapes
    work best, such as elbows or ditalini)

Sauce:

2–3 tablespoons olive oil

½ large onion, chopped

14 cloves garlic peeled and finely minced

Red pepper flakes (to taste)

2 ripe tomatoes, chopped and seeded

1 cup reserved pasta water

½ cup red table wine

1–2 heaping tablespoons dried oregano

1 (16-ounce) can chickpeas (also called garbanzo beans), rinsed

Salt and pepper, to taste

Grated Parmesan cheese for topping

Fill a large Dutch oven with water and add salt (to give the pasta flavor). Bring to a boil, then pour in pasta and cook according to box directions. Cook to taste (I prefer *al dente,* so I use the shortest indicated cooking time), then drain and set aside, reserving 1 cup of the liquid for the sauce.

Meanwhile, in a large enamel saucepan, pour in just enough olive oil to cover the bottom of the pan and heat over medium heat. When the oil is hot (you can put a small droplet of water in to see if it sizzles, but make sure you stand back so you don't get splashed), add the onion and stir until it is translucent. Next add the garlic, red pepper flakes to taste (start with ½ teaspoon), and chopped fresh tomatoes. When tomatoes start to break down and the mixture begins to look like a sauce, pour in the reserved pasta water. Add wine and the herbs and bring to a boil. Reduce to a simmer and let it thicken a bit. Add the chickpeas. Salt and pepper to taste.

Add the pasta to the sauce mixture. Combine gently, then place in your prettiest pasta bowl; a presentation that is aesthetically pleasing will give your spirits a lift. Top generously with grated Parmesan cheese and serve.

Simplicity!

✓ Pare down your possessions.

✓ Simplify your thoughts.

✓ Weed out negative relationships.

✓ Cook simple foods.

✓ Think of how you can simplify all areas of your life.

9

Caffè e Biscotti: Create Self-Enhancing Rituals for Well-Being

It is not fit that I should give myself pain, for I have
never intentionally given pain even to another.

—Marco Aurelio

I N THE LATE AFTERNOON, the time when people in other parts
of the world are just getting out of work, rushing home to walk
the dog, or driving through a fast-food chain, four silver-haired
gentlemen dressed in slightly outdated suit jackets (that used to
represent their Sunday best) sit leisurely around a little square sidewalk
table playing cards outside a café in Napoli. Bathed in the warm glow of
a slow-setting sun, one of them deals. Three onlookers stand motionless
as they study the players' hands and eyes, then hold their breaths for the

next move. A waiter comes out of the café with a small plate of biscotti and a tray of tiny espresso cups that are frothing at the top. A bubble of hushed anticipation envelops the scene as each man puts cards to chest just long enough to scan the offerings, approve of the *merenda* (afternoon snack), and turn his attention back to the serious business of pleasure. Voices gradually begin to rise and fall, spliced every now and then with a roar of laughter and then quieting back down to an almost sacred whisper. Any observer could easily sense the thrill of suspense, the *allegria* (cheer), the merriment in camaraderie, the joy of a *spensierato pomeriggio* (carefree afternoon). But on an ordinary afternoon in Napoli, it is not so easy to detect the hardship and adversities that have peppered the personal histories of those card players. One lost his wife just six months ago; another lost his granddaughter to a brain tumor; yet another has been out of work for years and struggles to make ends meet each month. Yet in the reassurance of a predictable feel-good ritual, life marches on for each of them, with dignity.

In Neapolitan life, it is a given that life changes and loss happens. An acceptance of "what is" frees one from a lifelong attachment to trauma. You pick up and go on; that is the only choice. Or as my relatives say when flanked by difficulty, "*Che ci posso fare?*" ("What can you do?"). It doesn't mean you are unaffected. It means life needs to be lived *now*.

The saving grace in turbulent times is being able to look forward to that next late afternoon of caffé and biscotti, the next carefree game of bocce with good friends, even *un'oretta* (hour or so) to sit on the front stoop and make small talk with neighbors who pass by. The Italian tradition of small pleasure rituals is the antidote to emotional upheaval. This predictable pattern in one's daily rhythm is like the netting that reassures a tightrope walker. Napoli, thought of by many as Italy's most vibrant city of contrast, chaos, great cuisine, and *amore* (love), exemplifies how feel-good, simple rituals elevate the soul.

Roman Emperor Marco Aurelio believed that our thoughts create happiness, and we should guard against thoughts that do the opposite.[1] Putting yourself in situations that make you feel good will also keep your thoughts on the right track to happiness.

Persistence leads to triumph. As you move forward through adversity, continuous feel-good rituals will keep you from wanting to give up. They remind you that life is still good and you are still an important part of it. Perhaps you've had to change locations, conduct a job hunt in your senior years, or deal with new fears and loneliness because of your loss. Don't waste time wishing that none of this ever happened to you; just begin to do things that make your life feel better right *now*. Consistently engaging in experiences that bring happiness will make a difference.

Keep in mind, not all behaviors geared toward feeling good are good for you. Some may even lead to worse states of mind. Excess alcohol, recreational drugs, overeating, and smoking are just some of the destructive "rituals" people risk turning to after loss. Positive feel-good rituals leave no ugly withdrawal effects. Quite the opposite. They will give you a sense of triumph over your difficulties.

Take the Plunge into Pleasure

Try this exercise and see if it makes a difference for you, as it does for me: Imagine that you are standing before the inviting emerald waters of the Amalfi coastline. You are overheated from the midday summer sun. Your skin is baked and you feel like you are about to faint from heat exhaustion. You stand at the edge of a rock cliff longing to dive in, but notice yourself hesitating. You don't relish that first shock of coldness you would feel if you were to take the plunge. Your choice is to stay uncomfortably hot, or take action that will refresh you if you are able to get past your initial fears. You decide to override your self-doubt and let your instincts lead you to what is best for you. You dive in. The refreshing waters envelop your body, invigorate you, and make you feel like a brand-new person. Even your mood has been refreshed. When you come out of the water, you have a new perspective.

There are times we must go ahead and act, despite our fears. Now may be the time to just *dive in.* Take active steps to make your afternoons relaxing, your mornings sacred, your evenings reflective and filled with gratitude for the gift of another day well-lived. Small pleasure rituals can help you to clear out the weeds that keep your life's garden from fully blooming. Sadly, most of us live on automatic pilot and take certain things for granted. No more. You are now being called to build a new life with the resources you have at your disposal. Make it resemble the person you are now. Perhaps wiser, more seasoned, stronger, more courageous. Although you may no longer have that once-important part of your life, think of the void that loss creates as a cup that is ready to be refilled with new experiences and opportunities for bliss.

Now is the time to make the changes that reflect your newfound strengths and the truth of who you really are. You may have been tolerating "friends" who don't treat you well. Find new ones. You may have always wanted to quit the job you hate and find one that you know you'd be happier in. Start looking. You may have always longed to have fun but have been too busy to build a social life. Schedule nonnegotiable social time once a week.

How we react to adversity will determine if we arrive at a better place.

After regrouping in the *lascia stare* phase, you now have the strength to take gentle actions that move you forward into the next phase of your life. Begin to actively counter the impact of your loss with daily thoughts of appreciation, rituals of pleasure, and self-enhancing statements. Marco Aurelio wrote in his *Meditations* (which were essentially letters to himself on how he aspired to marry the philosophy he believed in with his daily actions), "Think not so much of what thou hast *not* as of what thou hast, and reflect how eagerly they would have been sought if thou hadst them not."[2]

No matter how great your losses, behold every wonder that is still within your reach! Don't let these gifts be obscured by getting stuck in heavy grief forever. Allow yourself to gradually lighten your heart again. Let your actions help you do that. This does not mean that you will forget about who or what you have lost. Integrating whatever insights you have gleaned from your situation will move you forward in a meaningful way. Plan for nonnegotiable pleasure routines. Notice how much you love smiling again, you love cooking, going out for an ice cream cone with friends, or cuddling up with your kids or grandkids to watch a video. Yes, life is still good, and you want to keep loving it. Here are some suggestions:

- ✓ Take a daily pause for some great music and a dance around your living room.
- ✓ Plan a weekly date with a "true" friend to grab a rich cup of espresso at an outdoor café.
- ✓ Schedule a regular game of checkers outdoors or indoors with one of your kids.
- ✓ Take a long, uncharted drive along the back roads to enjoy the fall leaves.

✓ Start a ladies' (or men's) ice-cream cone night out.
✓ Enjoy a large pot of tomato sauce filling the kitchen with its rich aroma that you and your family make together.
✓ Organize a dog-walking group with owners of similar breeds.
✓ Start or join a monthly book club at your library.
✓ Coordinate a yearly potluck at your house of worship.

Look at your life circumstances as they are right now. What pleasure rituals can you build into your life? Plan out daily, weekly, monthly, and yearly pleasure habits, and you will begin to thrive once again.

The Importance of Pleasure When Getting Through Loss

Grief researcher George Bonanno observed that despite initial difficulties following trauma, the most resilient people displayed a tendency to continue social interactions, display positive emotions, and engage in generative experiences (such as exploring new activities or new relationships following their loss).[3] Positive feelings can help reduce the stress associated with adverse events, or even reverse negative feelings. Purposely creating situations each day that summon up good feelings and laughter can motivate you to keep on a path to a full and wonderful life after loss. Sometimes you will notice periods when grief revisits you, even after you think you are feeling better about things. That is perfectly normal. Try to guard against letting those periods go on too long, though. It is easy to get sucked back into the inertia of sadness, when your real purpose is to be present-oriented and live a vibrant live right now. It will take determination and small but purposeful actions. You can do it, and as your own best friend you owe it to yourself to follow through. I am not suggesting you deny your grief, but it can be helpful to put your sadness on "pause" every once in a while and give yourself a break. Often if you put sad thoughts out of your mind and immerse yourself in an activity that cheers you up, your sadness begins to lighten all on its own. Pleasure heals. Good times heal. Smiles and laughter, wherever you can get them, is the Italian prescription for a *dolce vita*. If you'd like to find out more about my prescription for a *dolce vita*, or to purchase that book, feel free to visit my website: http://raeleenmautner.com.

Do It Anyway

Doug, a young widower with no children, had no choice but to accept a transfer to his architectural firm's California office. He knew that if he turned down this opportunity, he might not find another job in this depressed economy. He'd relied on his friends and family as a base of social support since his wife died; now he had to leave them. It seemed like he had completely lost the life he once knew. The void of loneliness really hit him hard at first. Making friends never came easy to Doug; it took a long time before he felt he could trust people he didn't know. One night after work he was reading the local paper and decided to push himself to go to a lecture on the work of Renaissance architect Brunelleschi. Engrossed in the lecture, he hadn't noticed a woman next to him who was speaking Italian to her mother. At one point she turned to Doug, and, in very heavily accented English, asked him the English meaning of something the lecturer said. She smiled broadly as Doug made various attempts to explain using even more English words that she wasn't familiar with. They both began to giggle at their mutual attempts to understand each other. That sound of her carefree laughter felt like the levity Doug had been missing since he first moved to California. After introducing herself as Cinzia, she, her mother, and Doug ended up going for an ice cream after the lecture, and Cinzia's mom invited Doug for a simple *cena* (supper) the next night.

At that dinner, it occurred to Doug that he had been looking only at the bad features of living so far away from home. He realized that he was capable of creating his own happiness by the experiences he created for himself. He noticed how Cinzia's mom sang when she prepared their meal, and how upbeat Cinzia was as she set the table, placing each dish down as if she were laying gold before a king. The two seemed so blissful from the simple activity of preparing supper for a guest, nothing but the pleasure of that moment mattered.

After that insight, Doug began to change his life. He spotted a little coffee shop on the corner on his way to work and decided that from now on, his breakfast would be more than a couple of slices of bread with a little jam thrown on top as he ran out the door. Instead he would treat himself to a caffè latte and brioche every morning at the café. That was pleasure ritual number one. Soon that led to his becoming friends with the barista and looking forward to the lighthearted banter they exchanged every morning. He started to make other friends there as well and could count on breakfast time as a time for a smile and a few laughs.

Doug's second pleasure ritual was to learn how to surf. He had never surfed in his life; the waves on the East Coast never seemed to get higher than his waist, but he always thought about surfing when he saw people surfing in California on TV. Now he was here, so what was stopping him? For the next three months, Doug took a surf lesson every Saturday morning. He never could have imagined how much fun it was and how hard he could laugh, even when he fell off the surfboard, which happened less and less as time went on. Through surfing, Doug's social life filled out naturally. He would find himself in conversation with other people about the best boards or other related equipment to buy. His newfound love of surfing began to extend into other water sports, too.

Doug's third pleasure ritual was to go back to his house of worship on Sundays. He hadn't done so for years, but he remembered how calm he always felt when he went to church as a kid. The glow of the candles, the hypnotic smell of burning incense, the inspiration he would get from the sermons. Going back to church became like a weekly meditation for Doug, and it was a way to start his week with serenity and inner peace. His fears and doubts regarding how he would adapt to his transfer soon began to fade away.

Think and Say Good Things About Yourself

Italy's cultural philosophy is to put your best foot forward. This idea really stems from a dignity and self-pride in what you do, how you carry yourself, and how you look. It all matters in reviving your passion for life. This is not the same as conceit, but cloaking self-deprecation in a veil of false modesty is simply not done in Italia. That serves no one. The research shows that "self-enhancement" or positive biases toward oneself can be beneficial when it comes to overcoming loss and getting through grief. Saying positive things to yourself about yourself is even associated with lower cortisol levels, which are indicative of less stress.[4] Sometimes self-enhancement can be interpreted as being narcissistic and can certainly annoy others if carried to an extreme. But building up your self-esteem through honest self-enhancing affirmations during times of adversity can help to minimize the impact of your crisis.

This is not about acting superior, but about reassuring yourself, just as you would your very best friend or son or daughter if any of them were going through difficulties and you were the one they turned to.

What has hardship caused you to do or learn that makes you most proud of yourself? When I asked that question of Joseph, he admitted that he had never thought he would be able to get back out and into the dating scene after losing his wife of thirty-five years. Initially he was so nervous he would shake when he went to a singles dance. Before long, he began to relax and enjoy himself, which even sparked a new interest in taking ballroom dance lessons.

Roxanne was proud of the way she learned to draw personal boundaries and not be such a people pleaser anymore. After her husband Bob passed away, Bob's brother and his wife expected they would keep their old pattern of eating Sunday dinner at Roxanne's house. Roxanne quietly went along with it, but this routine now kept her from getting out and starting her own life over.

One Sunday, months after Bob died, Roxanne was sobbing over an old photograph when the doorbell rang. Brad and Margaret stood at the door, puzzled. They wondered why she had forgotten their dinner date. They thought it was strange that the table was not set. They demanded to know why.

Roxanne could have done her usual and just acquiesced. She could have apologized profusely and asked them to have a seat, and she could have whipped something up in a hurry, but something told her that since the playing field had changed, it was time for her to change, too, and express how she really felt. She needed to set limits to keep herself from situations that drained her energy and to choose experiences that would really bring her joy.

"I am sorry," she said, "but I will not be the Sunday chef anymore. I want to have some time to recharge my own battery. And maybe start going out. I hope you can understand that this is the way it has to be for me now."

Initially Roxanne's sister-in-law was offended, but she eventually came to respect Roxanne's new boundaries. Roxanne was able to feel good about putting herself first for once and defending her own well-being.

It is not selfish or narcissistic to defend your well-being and build yourself up in place of putting yourself down. Self-enhancement statements, and actions such as pleasure rituals, are healthy strategies that make you strong and make your life enjoyable again.

Put together a list of your accomplishments along with some photos or magazine pictures or sayings to keep you encouraged. Make these into a collage. Don't be shy about acknowledging what you have accomplished in the wake of your loss. If you had to move from your home, acknowledge that you are now an expert on the moving process, mortgages, rents, moving companies, whatever it is. If your neighborhood has been devastated by a storm, acknowledge how proud you are to have offered a helping hand to others, even when your own home suffered damage. Perhaps your loss has given you the courage to reach out to a support group whereas before you never thought you could. That is an accomplishment, too.

Take a few moments to take inventory of the skills you have gained in the process of making it through your crisis. You may have survived a night of relentless sobbing only to wake up with a smile; you may have gathered up the courage to ask people for help when you need it; you may have devised some concrete plans to get retrained, start your own business, or find a date online. You may have overhauled your eating habits and feel physically better than ever now. Always acknowledge the strides you have made. Upon reflection, you will realize how far you have already come.

Here are some ways that you can make self-enhancement a regular part of your life. Do a number of these each day, and watch how you begin to come out of the tailspin of confusion that your loss has brought about.

- ✓ Once a week, make or order a three-course gourmet meal, and you decide who you want to share it with. This will quickly build confidence in reestablishing a social life. My personal preference is Southern Italian cuisine. Start with antipasto, a primo of pasta with a light tomato sauce, and a grilled piece of fish topped off with an arugula salad with a bit of lemon juice and extra-virgin olive oil. Some fruit for dessert and a friend or two to eat with, and you will have a pleasure ritual fit for a queen or king.
- ✓ Write that book or poem, or those song lyrics that you have always wanted to write. Enjoy the process thoroughly. Dare to submit your work for publication, if that is what you have always dreamed about, or explore all the new options for self-publishing.
- ✓ Make Fridays your comedy movie night. Pop some corn, rent an old comedy, and have a friend or two over for some belly laughs.
- ✓ Put on your favorite music and let yourself go crazy. Sing in front of the mirror with a makeshift microphone, dance like a fool, get your body jumping like a jumping bean. Chances are you will start to laugh so hard you may end up rolling on the carpet.

Start to Enjoy Your Life Again— Beginning Today

The time has come to consider how you want your life to be from this day forward. You will no doubt want to keep some familiar aspects of the past as your foundation, but it is also important to add new activities, interests, friends, and fun times. Perhaps you want to start all over from scratch with a second career, or rekindle a dream you let go of long ago. By allowing yourself to go for it, you will rebuild your confidence and begin to leave the hurt and sadness behind. From this dark period of sadness you will begin to see the light of your personal renaissance, just on the horizon.

How about joining me vicariously in one of my favorite feel-good rituals—*caffè e biscotti* (coffee and a cookie). Here is my recipe for simple Limoncello Biscotti, to be enjoyed with a *bel espresso* (great coffee), a good friend, and as part of your self-enhancing makeover.

Limoncello Biscotti

MAKES APPROXIMATELY 4 DOZEN

Biscotti literally means "baked twice," but I bake them only once, preferring a softer cookie, with a bit of a sweet glaze on top. My family always loved this variation on my mother Rachele's recipe. I hope you will, too. Enjoy!

Biscotti:

1 stick butter (slightly softened at room temperature)

¾ cup sugar

2 eggs

1 teaspoon lemon extract

2 tablespoons limoncello (imported from Italy)

2 tablespoons grated lemon zest (not the white pith)

2 cups flour

1½ teaspoons baking powder

Pinch salt

⅔ cup chopped nuts of your choice (optional)

Glaze:

1 cup confectioners' sugar

2 tablespoons limoncello

Lemon juice, as needed

To make the biscotti: Preheat the oven to 350°F. Cream the softened butter with sugar. Beat in the eggs until smooth. Add lemon extract, limoncello, and grated lemon zest. Stir in flour, baking powder, salt, and nuts (if using). Mix ingredients well with clean hands. Lightly flour a cutting board or clean area of your counter, and divide the dough into two balls. Roll each ball into two long rolls, about 15 inches long. Place each roll on a nonstick cookie sheet and lightly press the top to flatten. Bake until golden, about 25–30 minutes.

To make the glaze: Combine confectioners' sugar, limoncello, and lemon juice as needed to form a thin, glazelike consistency.

When biscotti rolls are cool, use a rubber spatula to spread a thin layer of glaze on top and slice into ½-inch diagonals.

Saggezza—
Let Wisdom Guide You

The function of wisdom is to discriminate between good and evil.

—Marcus Tullius Cicero

WISDOM IS ABOUT GAINING INSIGHT on how to live well, cope with difficulties, and avoid problematic situations where we can. Sometimes we gain wisdom naturally from our experiences; other times we find answers in the writings of the sages. As they say in Italy, *In affari che non conoscete, chiedete sempre consiglio* (When you are faced with the unfamiliar, always ask for advice).

Sometimes hardship begets wisdom. From our painful struggles can come valuable life lessons about how we need to live from now on. This new awareness is critical to turning the lemons you were handed into *limoncello*. Wisdom will give you the peace and confidence to reinvent your life to fit your present situation. Self-reinvention does not mean you have to wipe out everything about your past. You do have to accept, however, that life is never the same after loss. You will be different from here on in, as you should be. After all, you are entering a different phase in your life. It may be just as wonderful, or perhaps even more wonderful than before, but either way, it will be different.

Picture a delicate wine glass into which the finest red wine is poured. The wine takes on the shape of the glass. But what happens when the glass breaks? That wine is spilled, and the shape that once held it is never to be again. You are about to pour your life's wine into a different-shaped glass. Some elements of the glass and its contents will still be recognizable, and some will seem unfamiliar. You are now meant to have new adventures and opportunities. Let the wisdom of your recent insights guide your new life.

Read Materials That Inspire You

Another way to gain wisdom is to begin reading the books of classic philosophers and brilliant thinkers as well as sacred texts or books that really have inspired you in earlier times. Set aside time each day to read or reread these kinds of materials. It worked for Marina.

When Marina and several people in her department received their layoff notices, Marina was the only one who seemed to remain cool. Her coworkers couldn't figure this out. They panicked, understandably, as the jobless rate was the highest it ever had been. They knew that Marina hadn't yet found another job and that she was a single mom to three children, one with special needs. Someone finally asked her how she could stay so calm, not knowing if she would be able to pay her next month's rent. Marina quoted a line from her favorite ancient Roman philosopher, Marco Aurelio: "If thou art pained by any external thing, it is not this thing that disturbs thee, but thine own judgment about it."

Aurelio was wise indeed. Who is to say that those who were laid off in the above example won't quickly find another job? Who knows if the reason for the layoffs was because a better job is meant to show up? What we tell ourselves about our crises can make a big difference in our recovery process. Marina was just as alarmed as everyone else when the layoff notices were handed out. But Aurelio's philosophy reminded her that how she interprets her situation was an even greater threat to her peace of mind than the layoff itself.

Wisdom gives life meaning. It has been defined as the ability to choose "rightly" when making a decision—and there are a lot of decisions to be made following loss. It is the capacity to see the larger picture beyond your own circumstances. It is the desire to keep learning new things, socializing with good people, and taking yourself out of your own head once in a while. Age alone does not guarantee wisdom. Wisdom develops with insights that lead to definitive changes in personal growth.

Turning to the sages works at any age. Drawing from the ancient Italian philosophers allows me to get out of my own head and tap into different ways of seeing things. I can pick the brains of those who made it their life's intellectual pursuit to think rationally and make deep observations about human nature. I am transported to another world when I read the works of Dante, Petrarch, Aurelio, Da Vinci, and others. These wise figures feel like old friends. I turned to them in my darkest hours after the death of my husband, immersed myself in their words, and they didn't disappoint. Their words reminded me to avoid lingering too long in my sadness and to use my courage to move ahead. Their ideas were treasures to me, as were their examples.

You will no doubt have your own favorite literary sages. Turn to them when you feel you have nowhere else to turn. You don't have to take every word you read to heart, just read for overall inspiration.

Identify Your Favorite Sages and Apply Their Wisdom to Your Life

Here is a small sample of some of my favorite sages from whom I draw inspiration and motivation. Who are yours? Make note of them and keep their books by your bed stand.

Marco Aurelio (121–180)

Wisdom: Learn from the Major Figures in Your Life

Marco Aurelio, emperor of Rome from AD 161 to 180, took stock of what he learned from the key people in his life. He wrote that from his father he learned modesty and manly character; from his mother, piety and beneficence; from his great-grandfather, the importance of having good teachers; from his governor, to want little, work with his hands, and not meddle in others' affairs. He also named other people who strongly influenced his life and who taught him the best way to live.[1] I believe we learn valuable lessons that lead to our own personal development from the people who have played various roles in our life, good or bad. From the good, we remember what characteristics we want to emulate; from the bad, we remind ourselves what kind of negativity to weed from our personality.

Marsilio Ficino (1443–1449)

Wisdom: Eat Right

A humanist philosopher of the Italian Renaissance, Marsilio Ficino devoted an entire chapter in *De Vita Triplici* to avoiding black bile, the fluid associated with melancholy (a noun he used to describe himself). His advice was to avoid "heavy and thick wine," food that is hard, dry, too salty, or bitter. He also suggested no fried foods, no old cheese, and no immersing ourselves in negative emotions such as anger, fear, pity, idleness, sorrow, or solitude. Centuries later, research shows that negativity is associated with an increased risk of heart disease, and that nutrition has a powerful impact on our mental and physical well-being.[2,3]

When you find that your sad mood isn't lifting, take action. Pay extra attention to eating right and make your thoughts positive. While these days we don't turn to "heavy and thick wine" or food that is hard or bitter, we do often turn to sugar, caffeine, and alcohol to numb ourselves when we are upset. I don't have to tell you that those foods in excess wreak havoc on your health. I wish the tendency for good self-care were as automatic as is our tendency for self-neglect in times of trouble, but the reality is that we have to make a special effort to put our well-being first during difficult times.

You can also do what behaviorists call a "stop thought" when you feel yourself wallowing too long in negative thoughts. Simply picture in your mind a big red stop sign or a police officer yelling at you to STOP for speeding down the street. This will sober you up and snap you out of your "anger, fear, pity, idleness, sorrow, or solitude." Marsilio Ficino had it right: It is up to you to progress toward the new day that awaits you. By eating right, we can get there with a strong body and a fit mind.

Giovanni Francesco di Bernardone: St. Francis of Assisi (1181–1226)
Wisdom: Help Others

The son of a wealthy cloth merchant, Saint Francis renounced his own worldly ways, left his fancy clothes by the wayside to don simple rags, and begged in the streets for his food. He came to believe, as his famous prayer testifies, that it is only in giving to others that we ourselves receive.[4] There is a lot I like about this prayer. Regardless of its religious affiliation, its philosophy rings true for anyone who has recently gone through a crisis. There is a time for grieving our loss and a time to get out of our own heads and help others. Not only is volunteer work a good distraction, but it helps us to realize how much we are needed, how valuable our lives really are, and what a difference we can make.

Shortly after Tom's death, I spotted a tiny ad, through our state department for the blind, regarding an Italian man who needed help writing letters. I was in. It was something I had the skill to do (since I speak Italian), something that I would love to do (it is hard to find other native Italian speakers where I live so it would be an opportunity for me to continue to speak the language I love), and something that would make me feel productive and not just defined by my loss. It was one of the most rewarding experiences I have ever had.

You don't have to go through a formal agency to do volunteer work. In the little towns of Italy, neighbors help neighbors whenever the opportunity arises. Someone loses a loved one and the whole town pitches in to get the bereaved on the path to healing. If you have a sick neighbor you can sweep her driveway or take out the trash. If tragedy or natural disaster hits two towns over, call the nearest Red Cross and ask how you can help. Doing volunteer work when you yourself are going through crisis will make you feel like you have just taken a shot of *limoncello* for the soul.

Laura Cereta (1469–1499)
Wisdom: Always Keep Learning

Laura Cereta was a Renaissance-era humanist and feminist who was no stranger to loss. In 1484, at a young age, she married her merchant of Venice, Pietro Serina, who, like her beloved father, encouraged her intellectual pursuits. Their happy marriage lasted only eighteen months. Her scholarship and continued pursuit of learning were Cereta's antidote for grief. She lost the other man who played a major role in her life—her father—only three years later. Cereta is remembered for advocating for the rights of women to be educated and acknowledged as having intellectual and emotional gifts of value equal to those of men's. She strongly believed in the right of all people to be educated. In *Collected Letters of a Renaissance Feminist*, Cereta's words are quoted: "Nature imparts one freedom to all human beings equally—to learn."[5]

When sleep would not come easily, Cereta often studied and read through the night. While I don't recommend you go without sleep, reading about new ideas and gaining new knowledge can be a real respite for the soul. When you're going through crisis, you need to strike a balance between processing the loss, reconstructing the road that lies ahead, and giving your mind a break with some distraction. Reading can do all three. Immersing yourself in philosophical readings will allow a deeper way of thinking to displace dwelling on your loss. The right reading materials can stimulate your mind and keep you centered. Choose something that challenges your brain but is not so complex that you exhaust yourself by having to use a dictionary at every page. Steer clear of books that bore you. Italian philosophers give me courage and reaffirm my joy for life. I also love sacred texts and inspirational self-help books, like those of Valerio Albisetti and Piero Ferrucci.

Giovanni Battista Vico (1668–1744)

Wisdom: Life Goes in Cycles but Always Evolves

Giovanni Vico was trained in jurisprudence but spent his career as a professor of rhetoric at the University of Naples. Vico wrote about two distinct dimensions to human nature—reason and imagination. Put simply, he left us with the notion that civilization progresses in cyclical motion. For example, society goes from a primitive, even barbaric, state to a refined, intellectual state, and then this process is interrupted by a "ricorso" or a return to a more primitive state, although not the original one, but a more evolved state.[6] Our lives progress in the same way. We are reassured by Vico's ancient philosophy that we are not the only ones to have our lives disrupted by trauma, crisis, and loss. It is a familiar part of the human condition as reflected in whole cultures and societies. While human nature is set up to attain its full potential, the road is filled with setbacks—none of which, incidentally, are powerful enough to send us back to square one. All of them contribute to our continued refinement and personal evolution.

Reflect on the Wisdom of People in Your Life

Then, of course, there are your everyday cast of characters, whose examples—good or bad—make you wiser. Like Marco Aurelio, we, too, can learn so much from the people who have been influential in our lives. Here are a few examples of the wisdom I've acquired from those in my life:

✓ From my husband, Tom, I learned *the value of cheerfulness*. I learned that it is always better to face each day with humor than to whine or complain. Life really is just happier that way. Every evening when he came home from work he would greet me in his happiest voice. Never did he walk through the door angry or complaining. He brought true sunshine to my life for many years, and I now make an even greater effort to bring positivity to the lives of others.

✓ From my father, Marino, and my mother, Rachele, I learned *the importance of a social life.* There was never a week where our house wasn't filled with card-playing buddies, bocce friends, or just friends paying impromptu visits. I learned how to build a network of friends with whom to get out and do things, especially when I was tempted to keep myself cloistered forever. My dad is now ninety-two and still loves to play bocce, cards, and pool. He still likes to dance, golf with my son, and cook for his friends. His social connections pulled him through when Mom died, and from him I learned the importance of maintaining social ties.

✓ From my grandfather, Domenico, I learned *the virtue of altruism.* Pop was a shoemaker who gave shoes and slippers to anyone walking by his store who looked like they needed them. He would give his merchandise away for free—not that he was so wealthy that he didn't need to earn a living, but because he believed he was wealthy in other ways: in the riches of a close-knit family. Thus, the least he could do was spend his life trying to put a smile on others' faces and give them those little gifts that meant so much to them.

✓ From Nonna Angelina I learned to *make mealtime a sharing time.* I learned that good food should be served in good company to make the experience complete. Angelina grew her own grapes for wine, her own figs (which required burying in the winter); she made her own sausage, bread, jam, and pickled vegetables from her garden. Best of all, she shared her gift with the entire neighborhood, because she believed the food tasted even better that way. From Nonna Angelina I learned that cooking can cheer me up, and having others over to enjoy it is a bonus.

✓ From my close friends (you know who you are) I learned *the importance of being there.* From my friends I learned how much it could mean to others going through crisis to have someone stand up for them, or organize things that they are too confused to organize. I am now more aware of that and look for opportunities to "be there" for others.

✓ From raising my children I learned *the necessity of letting go.* I love being a mother, despite the challenges and rocky roads that all parents have to deal with from time to time. Eventually I came to realize that letting our kids make their own mistakes is necessary and positive. Letting go is even more important when you are moving through loss and have no choice but to move forward.

What have you learned from the important people in your life? Write these philosophies out in bullet points to fit on one page, and put this sheet where you will see it often. Let what you learned from your relationships fuel your movement forward.

The hardships that befall us are not our fault; it is nothing we brought upon ourselves. We never expect bad things to happen to us, yet they are just as likely to affect us as anyone else. Remember the *ricorso,* the going back to a new beginning, not square one, as an even more evolved person able to live an even more passionate life. What will you do with your new beginning? I don't know about you, but I want my personal renaissance to be the best part of my life to date.

Sorridere e Mollare:
Smile and Let Go

*Ridi sempre, ridi, fatti credere pazzo, ma mai triste. Ridi anche
se ti sta crollando il mondo addosso, continua a sorridere.*
Always laugh, laugh, let others think you are crazy, but never sad.
Laugh even if the world around you crumbles, continue to smile.

—Roberto Benigni

CTOR ROBERTO BENIGNI, playing a character who is a professor of poetry, lectures passionately about the importance of being happy in the 2005 Italian film *La Tigre e la Neve.* "If you want to transmit happiness," he tells his students, "you have to be happy. When you want to transmit suffering, you have to be happy. Be happy. Everyone suffers. Be happy!" Just watching the passion with which he urges his students not to be bland makes you want to stand up, throw your arms up to the sky, and declare, "Yes, I am happy!" Happiness is often born from the decision to be happy, despite our suffering.

Benigni's character also tells his students, "Poetry is not outside, it is inside of you. If you want poetry, look in the mirror." My friend Ignazio was like walking poetry as he ambled toward me with a wide semi-toothed smile and arms outstretched. This octogenarian's charisma resembled the innocence of a joyful schoolboy. We both sighed with delight as we embraced in the Piazza San Pietro in Vatican City with the four rows of Tuscan colonnades as our backdrop. Pigeons flapped around our feet, people from all parts of the world walked by speaking their native tongues, but Ignazio stood firmly planted as he gripped my shoulders, kissed both my cheeks, and took a step back to examine me approvingly. His beaming face gave more the impression of a dashing Roman soldier than of an old man who had just been diagnosed with terminal cancer. His eyes crinkled at the corners when he smiled, and his lips seemed to stretch on for miles, barely leaving any space for cheeks. As always, it was an unpretentious smile from a man who accepted harsh realities as fully as he celebrated life's bliss. This celebratory reunion was the only thing his mind and heart were focused on at the moment. That smile was a powerful, authentic treasure that I will never forget.

Let Your Sorriso *(Smile)* Create Calm

In her book *Women & Beauty*, Sophia Loren commented on the mysterious allure of Da Vinci's smiling *Mona Lisa*. By most beauty standards, the face alone is not compelling, yet her smile has undeniably captivated our imagination for centuries. Loren decided to go to the Louvre to take another look at the painting so she might be able to relay to her readers some useful information on what really constitutes beauty beyond the traditional definition. To the critical eye, *Mona Lisa* is not the ideal of physical attractiveness, and yet our attraction to her is undeniable. After a good deal of reflection, Loren concluded that what makes *Mona Lisa* beautiful in the eye of her beholders is her captivating smile; it is a smile that reflects tranquility, "The kind of tranquility that comes with self-knowledge, and accepting yourself for who you are. The *Mona Lisa* appears to be telling you something with that smile; perhaps a secret that will change your life."[1]

The image of the *Mona Lisa*, the easygoing expression of the portrait's subject, Lisa Gherardini, can induce a similar calm in me. In the portrait, Gherardini's face is rested and her smile is soft as if lit from inside. This kind of inner beauty doesn't shine through when one is distraught.

Like Sophia Loren, I, too, am inspired by the aura of the *Mona Lisa* smile. No matter what goes on in my life, from here on in I want to be smiling through most of it, just as she does. Circumstances change. They can change for the better just as readily as they can change for the worst. Make an effort to start each day with a smile, knowing that something good can happen when you least expect it. Decide to sip the sweet nectar of each new day as it comes. When you go through tough times, realize that you are tougher still. Smile at your ability to *arrangiarti* (get by), no matter what. Smile at your growing confidence, your courage, and your newfound sense of calm. The more you smile, the more certain you will feel that all things will work out. A smile will lighten up your worries. A smile can reassure you that you, too, will make it, no matter what.

Smile to Feel Happier

Don't underestimate the powerful mood-changing effect in a smile. Have you ever been upset about something, and then a perfect stranger smiles as you pass on the sidewalk? Your negative mood instantly disappears. Perhaps you, too, can identify with waiting at a red light, looking anxiously at your watch or the light, hoping it will hurry and turn back to green so you won't be late for work. You glance over to the car next to you and the driver, also stuck in traffic, shrugs his shoulders and throws you a beaming smile. You can't help but smile, too. Even a simple ride up the elevator in a department store with someone who gives you a hearty smile can make you come out of that elevator feeling great. You have that same power to not only make someone else's day but to use your smile to change to make yourself happier. Smile frequently and you will see that this really works.

Use Your Smile to Create a Positive Mood

The idea of "fake it till you make it" has some validity in the cognitive behavioral field. Research shows that real physiological changes in the brain and other parts of the body take place when a person changes his or her facial expression.[2] A frown induces negative feelings; a smile does just the opposite. The facial feedback hypothesis in psychology states that facial expressions influence our emotions, as opposed to the other way around. Both Charles Darwin and William James were proponents of this philosophy.[3]

There is an Italian saying that goes, *"Il pianto non ripara i mali"* ("Crying doesn't fix the bad things in your life"). While it may be natural and even cathartic to cry when bad things happen, nonstop crying can also be destructive. The fact is, dreams are shattered all the time because life does not go as planned. However, trust that new dreams appear whenever you are ready. Let go of your sadness by smiling. Go out and give a smile to other people who need it. Such a simple gesture can create major change.

When you do smile, get your whole face involved. Smiles come in different categories, and not all smiles reflect happiness. Some people smile when they are nervous, frustrated, even angry. Scientists who have studied the anatomy of a smile found they could distinguish a genuine smile of happiness by the involvement of the muscles around the eyes, or contraction of the orbicularis oculi muscles, a phenomenon discovered by French anatomist Guillaume Duchenne. Duchenne described the full-faced smile as expressing the "sweet emotion of the soul," as opposed to the kind of smiles that maintain a facial inertia around the eyes.[4]

Smiling and laughter help people who are grieving in two important ways: First, they help us adapt better to our crisis by providing a psychological distance from our own distress; and, second, they help enhance our social lives—as when we smile or laugh (in the Duchenne sense, with full facial involvement)—because smiling evokes positive feelings in others as well as in ourselves. Insincere smiles or polite laughter just don't cut it. When the orbicularis oculi muscle was involved in the smiles of those who were grieving, they had more positive outcomes six months after their loss than did those who did not allow themselves to smile and laugh.[5]

As Ignazio and I walked over to the café right outside the piazza that day in Roma, he cried when he expressed his worries about leaving his elderly wife alone after he passed away, and he said he hoped that their children would make sure their mother would be okay when that happened. In Italy, the conversation is always more important than the destination, so we stopped walking for a moment. Ignazio sobbed for several seconds, then pulled out his handkerchief, wiped his eyes, and lit up again as he told me about his grandchildren's accomplishments. What I realized in that interaction is putting the smile before the feeling (like putting the cart before the horse) does not mean you are denying the reality. Quite the opposite; a smile makes reality more palatable and helps us to remember that life is always more than a string of sorrows.

Put Your Smile to Work for You

Zia Immacolata has been gone now for years, but what I remember most is the spontaneity of her smile. While hard at work in the fields she would spot me from afar, and her grin would let me know that all my troubles were about to fade away. Her smile was strong and unwavering. She had her hardships like everyone else, but she managed to smile through them. Because her smile made me so happy, I came to realize how my smile, too, can really turn someone's day around. It can make someone feel cared about, loved, or acknowledged in a uniquely human way. It can change someone else's life in an instant. When a person is down and out, the compassionate smile of another can often be the catalyst to a brand-new start. Put your smile to work for you and for others.

It is time to start telling your grief that enough is enough; it is time to turn the page. That doesn't mean you will forget what was—whether you lost a dream, your health, or a loved one. Now, however, is the time to give yourself permission to smile.

Think about what makes you smile most frequently. Perhaps it's the way your child's face gets covered with chocolate when he licks the frosting from the bowl. Perhaps it is the irony you are able to see in the toughest moments of your own life, and your ability to laugh at yourself. Let your smile start putting distance between you and sad memories. Cut your crying times short with the strength of a smile. Smile when you are happy and smile when you *need* to be happy. All things in nature grow, blossom, then die away, and it is impossible to stop this cycle. Keep your painful memories from overwhelming you. Keep the desire to turn back the clock dormant. Free yourself of regret, self-doubt, and fear as you straighten up your posture, smile, and move forward. There are times when your head has to take command of your heart. Make a decision to grace each day with a smile.

Here are just a few of some very Italian excuses for a smile:

- ✓ The *vendemmia:* the fall grape harvest in which neighbors get together to compare wines
- ✓ Participating in a *sagre:* a community festival constructed around local cuisine, a specialty of that region, music, dancing, and home-baked goods
- ✓ A tomato sauce that comes out perfectly
- ✓ A *passeggiata,* a stroll, through the main street of town, offering a chance to greet others
- ✓ A wedge of cheese, a loaf of good bread, and a glass of homemade wine

For more reasons to smile, go to: http://raeleenmautner.com.

Beyond Smiling

In addition to making sure you wear a smile, we have other tools at our disposal to help us feel more positive. Body posture can also affect our mood. If you hunch over and hang your head, your feelings will follow suit. The opposite is also true. Several times a day, check your posture and make sure your shoulders are back, your spine is straight but not stiff, your head is held gracefully high, and your pelvis is tilted forward slightly. Walk and talk with a spring in your step if you want your mood to follow suit.

The words you choose can influence your outlook on life. Certain phrases should be obliterated from your vocabulary. Instead of saying, "It is already too late for me," replace it with "I now have a new opportunity before me, and every day a reason to be happy." Don't say, "My life will never be good again," but instead tell yourself, "There are lots of things I like about my life right now—such as . . ." and list the people you care about, the activities that you still enjoy doing, and so on. Don't wallow in self-pity by saying, "I can't go on," but celebrate your new life by saying, "I can go on and I *will*. Life is a gift and I will not waste it being sad."

Your Smiling Assignment

You might think that an assignment to smile a certain number of times a day is ludicrous. Do it anyway. When I was going through my bereavement I wish I had read the words I am now writing for you. Smile even when you don't feel like it, and you will begin the necessary work of detaching from the pain of your loss. You will never break free of your trauma unless you begin to let go of your past, even if you have to push yourself to do it. When I lost Tom, I could never even imagine that I would ever again enjoy life. In my darkest moments, I remembered the sparsely toothed smile of my old friend in Rome and recalled how even between life's heartaches a space for joy can be found.

Leonardo da Vinci's *Mona Lisa* has one of the most debated expressions in history. Is she really smiling or is her expression more neutral? Because of her positioning and the use of light and shadow, Da Vinci very effectively spurred heated debates even centuries later. Some experts believe that the artist may have done this purposely. Don't leave room for debate when it comes to *your* smile. Make no mistake about it: A full sweet smile will lead to a lighter heart.

Parte Terza (Part III)

Reagire:
Begin to React

Sistemare la Casa: Organize Your Home and Your Surroundings

A ogni uccello il suo nido è bello.

To each bird, his own nest is beautiful.

—Italian proverb

ITALIAN HOMES ARE TYPICALLY KEPT CLEAN and organized and thus feel spacious even when living quarters are tight. At the end of the day, it is a pleasure to come home to and be able to relax in your welcoming home. You know where everything is and where you can find it at a moment's notice, because nothing is buried under anything else. Completing projects around the home will bring your confidence back and make you feel good when you look around your living spaces.

My friend David's house reflected an eerie stillness eight months after the death of his wife. The lifeless clutter reflected an upturned life that had been frozen in its tracks. Framed photographs of Linda, scattered throughout the house, were gathering dust. The sink was piled high with crusted-over dishes that filled the kitchen with their stench. Mounds of neglected paperwork were stacked high on the little oval table in the kitchen: recent medical bills, insurance statements, long white envelopes containing half-filled brown plastic pill bottles. There was a tiny clearing where David had pushed away the rubble to make space for his plate. The living room was strewn with his clothing— jackets, coats, and shoes just thrown to the floor until the next time they would be worn. A very old cat lay on one of the heaps that continued onto the couch. Heavy burgundy draperies were drawn, letting in only a thin stripe of sunlight. His depressing outer world was an expression of the sadness he felt inside. Absent was any desire to salvage the rest of his life and make it a good one.

David explained that he really didn't know how to clean house; his wife had always been the one to do so, and he wouldn't know where to begin. His perceived helplessness only compounded his depression.

"How long do you want to keep going like this?" I asked him. He looked puzzled. It hadn't occurred to him that he had any other choice.

Barbara, on the other hand, made so many dramatic changes when her marriage broke up that she nearly brought herself to the point of collapse. After finding out that her home would be going into foreclosure, she took a week off from work, scoured several newspapers a day to find a place to live, called credit card companies, banks, and other sources about salvaging her credit and getting some of her debt forgiven, and took on a job search so that she could make more money and afford to live in a community where she could feel safe.

The number of tasks on Barbara's to-do list soon began to outweigh her supply of energy, causing her to give up on everything. Daily good intentions soon turned into days of overeating, napping, surfing the Web, watching TV, and lying around in her pj's.

Both David and Barbara showed very common symptoms associated with the aftereffects of loss and personal trauma. Both reactions are nonproductive and will ultimately make you feel worse. It is not uncommon to neglect important aspects of our well-being—like good eating habits, a vibrant social life, clean surroundings, and stress reduction techniques—when we are adjusting to loss. You will come to the point, however, where you know you need to give yourself a gentle—or not so gentle—push to get up and reclaim your life. Restoring order to your home is a good place to start. It is also a very Italian antidote to a negative emotional state that you can't seem to pull yourself out of.

In *Women & Beauty,* Sophia Loren wrote about organization as a concept that sounded dull and full of obligation. Yet an organized home, according to this Italian icon, makes your life easier and more pleasurable. The freedom that comes with gaining control of your house chores can even make you feel more youthful. She suggests organizing for pleasure instead of avoiding what must be done, as David was doing. Loren believes that when we put off chores, we feel guilty and more stressed. She suggests turning housework into funwork by approaching tasks with "concentration, love, and patience" as well as engaging the help of others to lighten the load.[1]

While your loss may change your life forever, everyone's life is ultimately about change. Start to think of your setback as surmountable, and the changes you must make as doable. A million new possibilities await you. You will get clearer on everything you need to do when you begin clearing the clutter from your surroundings. That includes your home, your garage, your yard, your car, your workspace, and even the relationships, which, like weeds, have been choking the life out of you.

Cleaning Is Calming and Life-Affirming

Housework really gets a bad rap, but in fact housework can be therapeutic, especially when you are hurting.

The act of cleaning can make you feel tranquil. Donatella claims that cleaning out her cabinets and washing out her refrigerator de-stresses her when she is upset. When she's finished, she looks around at everything and smiles. Visual beauty—as in a lovely home—is also healing. Your home is your environmental artwork. It is the first thing you see when you get up in the morning and the last thing you look at before you close your eyes at night. You deserve to see beauty, regardless of your budget. So clean out the old, make room for the new, and feel hopeful about each new day to come.

The Italian Housework Solution

Post-WW II Italy fell onto hard economic times, which prompted many Italians to develop a frugal mentality and avoid extras like the latest cleaning tools and appliances. As it turned out, saving money alone did not explain why Italians resisted the latest housekeeping innovations. Housewares companies learned the hard way that time-saving devices that sold well in other cultures were a turnoff to Italians, who preferred to immerse themselves in their cleaning rituals at a slower pace, focusing on doing the job right, not doing it fast. Doing it right—the slow way—has benefits that go beyond the satisfaction that comes from having sparkling countertops. Housework can also serve as a reprieve from whatever ails you. And an added bonus: The aesthetic value of an uncluttered space will give you clarity of thought and peace of mind.

Use Housework as a Distraction

The Italians in my family taught me by example that housework can have a lulling, transcendent effect, not unlike meditation. The total involvement of body and mind in carrying out the tasks of home upkeep—from sweeping your front porch to washing dishes—can bring about a sense of well-being.

My relatives in Italy have very sparkly homes. The homes are modest and plunked along dusty ancient roads or stretches of farmland. Yet their dwellings seem spacious, airy, and beautiful. The process of maintaining them is uplifting and fun, especially when a few family members work in unison. Cleaning can be cathartic and much more productive than eating an entire half-gallon of ice cream to numb your pain. According to a Proctor & Gamble survey, Italians spend twenty-one hours a week on household chores, and they like to do them the slower, old-fashioned way.[2]

I remember washing dishes with one of my best friends only a few days after Tom's death. As we washed she would comment on the beautiful deep green color of the dish liquid. She put the bottle to my nose and invited me to smell its clean fragrance, then to listen to the trickling of water from the faucet as it filled up the wash bucket. We picked out the multitude of colors as we plunged our hands into the hot soapsuds. We noted the squeaking of the plates as we gave them a final rinse and arranged them on the dish rack. There is nothing more mundane than washing dishes, and, yet, for those few minutes, I escaped my grief.

Calabrian-born classical crossover singer Micheal Castaldo is known for saying: "Life is not a cup to be drained, but a measure to be filled."[3] You may have lost an important part of your life but it is time to start filling your measure back up. Getting rid of clutter gives you a better perspective on what you want to fill it up with.

Use Housework for a Daily Dose of Self-Esteem

Housework is free, it is good for your body and mind, and the end product of a beautiful home created by your two hands will make you feel valuable, confident, and proud. These are the feelings that will best nurture you right now. Imagine the satisfaction of opening your dresser drawers and finding everything right down to the very last sock. Imagine your pride as your closet displays its contents, making it easy to pick out what to wear, what fits, what makes you feel cheerful when you put it on. Imagine the floors sparkling around you, the photographs on the walls all cleaned and chosen for their ability to make you smile. Housework as mood therapy is a very Italian antidote to the blues.

How to Clean Your Sorrows Away, Italian Style

Italians resist automatic dishwashers, but even when they concede, you can be sure the dishes are prewashed anyway. They demand their washing machines go in cycles half as fast as the spin rate of machines in the United States, and they refuse to eliminate water-filled buckets in place of an "all-in-one" squirt mop. They place value in a slower, meditative process of cleaning.[4]

Logistically, there are many ways to clean house. Italians are not advocates of rigid rules or jam-packed to-do lists. It is actually fun to get creative when cleaning and organizing your home. Try out new products, new furniture arrangements, new storage ideas, and contemporaneously you will have started making your new life fresh and wondrous.

If you feel like it, you can clean and organize an entire space (the whole room or closet, for example) or a part of the home with a common theme (perhaps just the cabinetry in the kitchen or just the floors in the home), and allow the psychological effect of completing something energize you. Be realistic about how much time you will need to complete your tasks. Once you've chosen an area that seems easy enough to accomplish, start by discarding or donating any items you don't use and haven't used for a while. Then gather dust cloths, cleaning solutions (natural or commercial, see below), vacuum, mop, and trash bags in any combination that works for you.

Don't let your home reflect the inertia of loss like David's or the chaos of trauma like Barbara's. Rise up and freshen your dwelling. Here are some ideas to help you get started:

- ✓ One closet in the home. Start by discarding or donating clothing and accessories that you haven't worn in a long time, then wipe off the shelving, arrange clothes in the order that makes sense to you, and put a few natural cedar chips or a few drops of cedar oil in the corners of the shelves to keep moths away naturally.
- ✓ Basement: Because the basement covers a large area, divide the space into four, then do one area per session. Get rid of what you don't look at, and keep only that which you still use or love.
- ✓ Garage: Purchase racks for tools and bicycles. Get some inexpensive shelving for objects like gasoline containers, hose nozzles, and extra

outdoor bulbs. Keep the floor swept, the ceiling corners free of cobwebs, and the windows clean.

✓ Bedrooms: All mattresses and pillows should be aired out, shaken, or vacuumed. Open up the window for a few moments each day to clean the air. Keep bureaus dusted and free of clutter. Mirrors should be polished and floors free of under-the-bed dust clumps.

Natural Italian Cleaning Solutions

Italians are divided when it comes to commercial-brand cleaning products versus natural solutions for green cleaning. The latter are cheaper and nontoxic, and I personally prefer what my ancestors used. However, it is also true that commercial cleaning solutions are sold in Italy in containers that are up to 50 percent larger than in the United States because of the Italian propensity to clean so frequently. Use your favorite cleaning solution if you have one, or you can whip up the green mixtures that many tradition-loving Italians use.

White Vinegar

✓ In Italy, vinegar is used to prevent mold in shower stalls, and it can be mixed with baking soda to clean toilets and around drains in sinks. Don't use on marble, however, as acids will etch it.

✓ A cup of white vinegar per gallon of hot water can be used to clean floors. If you have pets, this is a great nontoxic option.

✓ You can also clean your windows and mirrors with white vinegar. Simply make a 50/50 solution of vinegar to water, put into a spray bottle or dip a soft cloth in, and wipe clean with a dry cloth. I use bits and pieces of old flannel shirts or pajamas.

✓ Put a full cup of white vinegar into your toilet bowl. Add a quarter of a cup of bicarbonate of soda, and when it is done fizzing, scrub away the stains with a toilet brush.

Lemon and Lemon Juice

✓ Try slicing a lemon in half and using it as a cleaning tool to make the metal fixtures of your sink sparkle; avoid getting it on marble because acid will etch it.

✓ Sprinkle a little table salt on a sliced half of lemon to get rid of stubborn stains on your countertops (avoid this on surfaces that scratch easily, like marble).

✓ Remove stains from your cutting boards by rubbing a halved lemon across them, then letting that juice sit for twenty minutes before washing it off with a cloth.

Olive or Lemon Oil

I like to put a few drops of olive or lemon oil on my dust cloth and polish my wood furniture. It leaves a nice subtle shine and a refreshing fragrance.

Hydrogen Peroxide

A traditional Italian cleaning solution is ½ cup of hydrogen peroxide to 1 cup of water. Put it in a spritzer bottle and clean your bathroom fixtures.

Boost Your Dish Detergent

An Italian tradition is to add some boiling water to the dishpan, to which is added a couple of capfuls of liquid detergent. Soak the dishes in there for fifteen minutes before washing. Make sure the water is cooled enough to avoid burning your hands before you wash and rinse.

Milk

The lactic acid in milk makes a classic cleaner for your silverware. Soak silverware in milk up to forty-five minutes and then wash with hot water and detergent. Rinse and polish with a soft cloth.

Scent Your Home Naturally

Take the peels of any citrus fruit and add to them a few drops of citrus oil to intensify the fragrance. You can also add a few leaves of fresh mint. Wrap a piece of gauzy cloth around the little bunch of peels. Place in a pretty plate in the bathroom or in other living spaces of your home.

Organizing your home will distract you from your problems, induce serenity, and beautify your surroundings. You are reclaiming the details of your life after loss. Be mindful to slow your own pace when house-cleaning, and, as you eliminate the toxins from your surroundings, you will also eliminate the "toxins" from your thoughts. Cleaning your home can signal a very important turning point in your psyche. There comes a time when you are no longer defined by being widowed, unemployed, sick, disabled, motherless, childless, marriage-less, or by anything else. You are not your loss, and you are not "less than" because of your loss. You have just created open airy spaces around you; now open up your heart to the beauty waiting to fill it up. The best way to claim victory after loss, is to renew your commitment to *live*.

13

La Sprezzatura:
Make the Difficult Look Easy

Functionality and beauty are the very essence of Italian
civilization. . . . This aesthetic pragmatism has its roots in
Italy's incomparable tradition of craftsmanship throughout
the ages and is still evident in the country's flair for design. . . .
—Peter D'Epiro and Mary Desmond Pinkowish in *Sprezzatura*

S ERGIO MADE CONVERSATION WITH STRANGERS seem more like
a reunion with long-lost high-school friends. He was dashing
in dark-rinse denim jeans, loafers, and a crisp untucked shirt,
the color of the Italian Dolomites after a fresh winter snow-
fall. Everyone who found their way to his *ristorante* (restaurant) in the
Tuscan region of Italy came out believing they had been led to his estab-
lishment by *Il Destino* (Destiny). "Simple elegance" would describe the
atmosphere of the *ristorante;* it tickled patrons' anticipation of culinary magic. The air was filled with the masterpieces of classic Italian

composers and the fragrances of uncorked fresh wine and simmering sauces just waiting to be drizzled over homemade pasta. Sergio effortlessly engaged everyone from wealthy international businessmen to giddy *innamorati* (lovebirds). With arms outstretched and a deep voice that emanated warmth, Sergio made each patron feel at home, and he made sure not to offend anyone, not even when he was dragged into an argument about the topics most Italians get heated up over—politics and the economy. He was masterful in his ability to politely ease his way out of any potential disagreement and onto a new discourse that was less controversial and evoked good feelings. Sergio's aplomb set the tone for an evening of good cheer.

Until a year ago, Sergio's wife, Mara, would be right by his side, welcoming guests and signaling to the maître d' which table a particular client preferred. Mara had been Sergio's longtime partner in business and in love, but a long, dragged-out divorce trial resulted in Sergio losing nearly everything he had—including the *ristorante.* Mara was now his boss, and Sergio was told that if he wanted to continue to see his children he had to accept the situation and find a way to make peace with his new circumstances.

Sergio's biggest challenge was to accept reality, let his frustration go, and still find a way to live with this situation so that his life would not be difficult. It was no easy feat, but he kept his tranquility and reminded himself of his priorities. First and foremost was continued access to his children (the loves of his life), his clients, and his ability to love, laugh, eat, and be satisfied with another day lived well.

Sergio's ability to handle his challenges with what would appear to be relative ease exemplifies what Count Baldassare Castiglione referred to as *la sprezzatura* in his classic 1528 book, *The Courtier.* Loosely translated, *la sprezzatura* means making the difficult look easy. *La sprezzatura* gives grace to one's actions and joy to one's onlookers. In fact, Castiglione believed that "the exhibition of art and study so intense, destroys the grace in everything."[1] The coping skills we need to learn following loss should be learned so well they become effortless and allow you to carry on with your life with dignity.

Wonder is an emotion that is incompatible with sadness. Accomplishing something difficult with such adroitness that you make it look easy inspires awe in others as well as in you. In *The Courtier*, Castiglione revealed his philosophy about how a true renaissance gentleman should behave, emphasizing the importance of knowing how to do certain skills so well, that you "de-price" or downplay the effort it takes to carry them out. It takes practice to give the appearance of an effortless mastery of skill in any area of your life. Castiglione believed that observers feel inspired when exposed to such artistry of behavior, and so it was the courtly or gentlemanly (or womanly) thing to strive for. *La sprezzatura* can be an important tool for getting your confidence back.

Put Some Tasks on Automatic Pilot

Sergio was determined to let his life flow smoothly, despite his change in status and the personal turmoil brought about by such a public court case. He got through that crisis by becoming so proficient at running the restaurant that he could operate on "automatic pilot" and free up his energy for other areas in his life, like strengthening relationships with the people he loved. The concept of *la sprezzatura* can be viewed temporally as a predecessor of the more contemporary Italian emphasis on *fare una bella figura* (putting your best foot forward at all times).

While going through adversity, if we automate certain skills that we do so well that we don't even have to think about them, we can free up the emotional and physical resources we need to make changes that will move us forward.

What Castiglione referred to as *la sprezzatura,* cognitive psychologists refer to as *automaticity,* which is the ability to perform a task so well and with such little effort, that your attention can be on something else at the same time.[2] One example is playing a piece on the piano flawlessly, while holding a conversation with someone who just walked into the room. The research comparing expert and novice chess players shows that because of their greater experience in playing the game, experts can recall certain board patterns automatically, thus freeing up their energy to concentrate on other nuances of the game. Even if well trained, novices use up all of their mental energy trying to recognize the same patterns that experts see on the fly.[3] When you first learn to drive a standard shift car, there is a lot to have to think about: how to position your hands, which gears are appropriate for highway versus street driving, when to use the clutch, and so on. After getting used to the procedures, all of these steps come together without even having to think about them intentionally. Think of how much easier your life would be if you could put many of your everyday tasks on automatic pilot.

Put Positive Thoughts on Automatic Pilot

While automaticity of skills can be helpful when going through the process of rebuilding your life, emotional automaticity is the other side of the same coin, and equally necessary if we believe the research on happiness. Dwelling on the negative aspects of your crisis can keep you down and depressed indefinitely. The problem for many of us is that a negative bias in our thinking is more likely to be the stronger automatic thought habit. For example, we don't automatically think of the good that might come in the aftermath of our loss. We don't automatically remind ourselves about the magnificent experiences we can continue to enjoy, love, and appreciate. We don't automatically fill our heads with self-affirming positive affirmations. Usually, we do just the opposite.

Castiglione pointed out that *la sprezzatura*—making the difficult look easy—requires practice. He was of course referring to behavioral skills. For example, you get speedier at the once-unfamiliar task of using a new electronic gadget the more you do it. The more you use the various features, the easier it becomes. We can apply the same philosophy to practicing positive thinking. Thoughts, by the way, are the keys that unlock our emotions, and thoughts match up perfectly with their corresponding emotions. You cannot think a negative thought and feel happy anymore than you can feel happy while thinking of something dreadful. Both uses of automaticity—for productive actions and productive thoughts—can become your bridge to a life that is more satisfying than you could ever have imagined. Think of the aftermath of loss as a clean slate, which gives you the opportunity to redesign many aspects of your life. You didn't ask for the loss, nor did you want it, but the reality also brings with it new hope if you choose to think of it that way. Keep encouraging yourself as you pave the way forward.

How to Let Sprezzatura Ease You Through Crisis

A few months after Jennifer was diagnosed with multiple sclerosis, her boyfriend decided he couldn't stay in her life. He feared the possibility of having to be her caretaker one day and broke off their relationship.

Jennifer felt scared and betrayed. She had no idea what the progression of this disease would be like, and the person she thought she could rely on for support was gone. After plummeting into a period of initial distress, she figured out how to automatize the skills and talents she had to ensure that she would make it through tougher days when she would likely need more rest.

One of the skills that came most easy to Jennifer was organization. While she was still feeling well enough, she decided to reorganize her whole kitchen so that everything she needed would be easily accessible on days when she would find it hard to reach up to top cabinets or to open sealed jars. She placed all of her assist tools, like easy jar-opener devices, right in the drawer by the stove. She labeled the outside of the drawers so she would not get frustrated trying to recall where everything was. She bought a number of freezer containers so on days when she felt good she could make extra meals and store them in the freezer for days when she didn't feel well. When the kitchen was done, Jennifer proceeded from one room to the next until her whole apartment was more accommodating. She felt safer and more secure.

The Roman poet Orazio (Horatio) once said, "Adversity has the effect of eliciting talents which in prosperous circumstances would have lain dormant."[4] The ancient Romans believed that from adversity is born the strength that helps a person get through that adversity. Since your life changed course, you have probably discovered skills and talents you never knew you had. Use them to make your life easier while starting to rebuild your life. Doing what comes easily to you will build confidence as you get things accomplished despite your setback. How to get started? Take a skill inventory right now of things you do so well that you can practically carry them out while sleepwalking. Then figure out how you can use these "easy" skills to help make your life run smoothly while you face the tougher issues you need to address. When you are picking up the pieces after loss, you want your life to be easy. No one wants their short journey on earth to be a sentence of hard labor. Avoid the frustration of doing things that exhaust you. Now is the time to recover your strength and energy. Here are some examples:

- ✓ Romy did not expect to feel so useless upon her retirement. She became doleful thinking that she was no longer contributing to society. Then Romy picked up her knitting needles. She has knit so many sweaters over the years that she barely needs to follow the directions of a pattern. In a sense she knit her way out of a slump, while completing one sweater after another, to donate to the local nursing home. She felt calm while she knit, and proud of the results. She knit well and could watch her favorite shows at the same time. Instead of draining her energy, the task energized her.

- ✓ Mario's company transferred him to the United States, where the customs and traditions were as unfamiliar to him as was the geography. With thirty years of experience riding motorcycles, riding was second nature to Mario, to the point where he could take in the scenery while simultaneously riding safely. He used his advanced skill, which he did effortlessly, to help him learn his way around his new surroundings. On weekends he rode all day until the lay of the land became as familiar as an old friend.

- ✓ Joan has played guitar for many years. She often jams with friends when she is faced with difficult challenges. It gives her time to refresh and rethink. The night her father passed away, her guitar seemed to play itself even though she was doing the strumming. The melodies were soothing and life-affirming. She was able to reflect on her father and on her own process of grief and healing as she played.

Emotional Automaticity: The Dos and Don'ts

While developing the emotional skills to counter loss, you need to make positive thoughts become habitual, while at the same time blocking out automatic negative thoughts as soon as you become aware of them. What we refuse to dwell on is just as important as what we should dwell on. Psychologists say it takes at least three weeks to turn a behavior into a habit. For the next three weeks, zero in on practicing thoughts that promote self-encouragement, which bring with them good feelings. You can do this by repeating what psychologists call autogenic phrases (or positive affirmations in layman's terms). Contemporaneously, imagine all negative thoughts—thoughts that frighten, confuse, worry, dishearten, or create self-doubt—floating up in a helium balloon that goes so far away into the sky that you can no longer see it, and those thoughts are no longer part of your daily thought repertoire.

When you are traumatized by loss, sometimes professional help can be an important source of support until you are in a better place emotionally. Don't be afraid to ask for help when you need it, but neither should you expect that anyone else can get you to be fully committed to your own life again. Only you can do that, and, yes, it takes determination and persistence.

Rosemary, for instance, kept her house like a museum dedicated to her son Daniel, who died in the war. His room was kept exactly how Daniel had it before he went off to war. She would stand in his doorway each day and stare into the room, regretting how she did nothing to dissuade Daniel from joining the military when he told her of his decision. Then she would cry nonstop until her husband or one of her other children led her away and closed the door again.

Letting the negative fade away. Easing emotional suffering requires a decisive choice to eradicate all self-destructive thoughts. Rosemary's situation was tragic and traumatic, yet she kept retraumatizing herself by engaging in a daily ritual that made her feel even worse, until it became an automatic part of her day. For her own emotional survival, it was important to banish that ritual and replace it with positive feelings, life-affirming memories of Daniel, and gratitude for what she still had in her life, such as her husband and her other children. Only by stopping painful destructive habits would she be able to start rebuilding after loss.

Positive affirmations. Most of us are completely unaware of most of the thoughts that automatically run though our heads on a daily basis. In general, these thoughts are self-deprecating, not self-reassuring. Common thoughts that only intensify your suffering include "I don't think I can do this," "Why did I do that?" "If only I (did, didn't), then this might not have happened," "I will never make it." It is imperative that you wipe out the automatic flow of negative thinking by making new positive affirmations become automatic in their place. You have to catch yourself thinking those destructive thoughts to do this. Then replace them. Repeat your new supportive statements often throughout the day, until they become second nature to you. Here are a few examples:

✓ Things may not be the same, but different can be wonderful, too.
✓ I love and forgive myself for anything I think I could have done better.
✓ This may be the end of one segment of my life, but I still have many contributions to make.

For more examples of autogenic statements that work, please visit http://raeleenmautner.com.

Coping skills. Automatic coping skills will help you keep your calm in turbulent times. Instead of panicking when you have to make a decision you are feeling uncertain about, learn to approach your problems systematically until this procedure becomes effortless. You can systematize problem solving by first writing down the problem in very specific detail. Then list all possible solutions that come to mind, even if some of them seem far-fetched. Finally, choose one that makes the most sense and then go with it. If it doesn't turn out as you had hoped, you can always go back and work with another.

Automatize positive initial reactions. When something bad happens to us, we tend to automatically block out any thoughts that might help us to get through it. Instead of thinking that what has just happened will doom you forever, try telling yourself immediately when something bad happens that although this situation seems devastating, you will know how to get through it as you go along. And you really will, even if at first you can't imagine it.

Reactions you should not automatize. One of the first things that Gail talks about wherever she goes is that she is widowed. "Please put the groceries in a double bag," she told a supermarket cashier recently. "Since my husband passed away, I have to carry these alone." While Gail didn't intentionally try to seek sympathy from others, in effect she was automatizing her self-pity and her victim status. If you ever want to get your life back in all of its vibrancy, you must make victory—not defeat—your automatic motto. Take note that you probably *are* able to carry your own bags. If that is the case, then rejoice in the two strong arms you have! If you can do this, what else might you be able to do?

This is the way to think. An attitude of victory, not victim-ry, is the *only* automatic status to give yourself.

To cancel out the automaticity of defeat, try one or more of the following suggestions:

✓ Go an entire day without talking about your loss. Then make it two days, then an entire week. Become engaged in the parts of life that lie outside of your loss. Although what happened seems like your entire world, practice taking a more global perspective and get involved with the broader aspects of your life.

✓ Limit your rumination time. It is one thing to process a major life transition; it is another to keep your wound raw by revisiting it constantly and without resolution. By resolution, I mean every time you think about your "old life," you should find some part of it to smile about, some part of it to learn from, or some part of it that makes you strong. This is productive reflection, not debilitating rumination.

✓ Make an actual/ideal self chart. Take a sheet of paper and put a circle in the middle with your name in it. Let five or six lines radiate out of that circle, and at the ends of these subcircles place two smaller circles, of varying distance apart. The lines represent what you would consider the most important dimensions of your life (for example, finances, love, fitness, friends, and so on). Let the two smaller circles at the ends of these outward lines represent your "actual" and "ideal" status in each area. Some of the circle pairs will be closer together (for example, your "family" circle pair will overlap or even look like one circle if your actual relationships with your family are ideally where you'd like them to be); others will be farther away (for example, your "fitness" circle pair may have a greater distance between them if your fitness goal is far from where your current fitness level is). Next, in between your circle pairs, write steps for moving yourself closer to where you want to be—that is, for closing the gap between your actual-ideal status in each area. This is a very powerful exercise, reaffirming that you have a plan to make your life into what you now want it to be. If you'd like some help on how to draw this chart, you can find an example on my website: http:// raeleenmautner.com.

La sprezzatura as applied to loss recovery is about making good thoughts—which lead to positive feelings—automatic through conscious repetition. It is also about capitalizing on the physical skills that already come easily to you, and using them to get things done while conserving the energy you need to rebuild your life. Practice life-affirming thoughts and actions until they become so automatic that they come to you naturally and often. Begin talking only about what is in your life that you love right now, and about your current goals and dreams. Commit to becoming your own best friend and telling yourself all the reassuring things that one's ideal best friend would say in times of crisis. When you talk about the past, talk also about how fortunate you are to have had whatever it is you feel sad about losing. Practice joy, positivity, and happiness. Practice doing the best you can in every precious moment in which you can still take a breath. These are the most rewarding daily rituals you can cultivate.

14

Lavorare Sodo: Work Hard to Forget Your Troubles

Every moment . . . do what thou hast in hand with perfect and simple dignity . . . to give thyself relief from all other thoughts.

—Marco Aurelio

MARIO GIACOMELLI WAS A RENOWNED Italian photographer whose brilliant black-and-white photographic portraits of courageous rural families laboring in the fields of postwar Italy illustrated that hard work leaves no room for fear. These compelling and emotional images of everyday Italian life against a backdrop of adversity reveal extraordinary expressions of human dignity, integrity, and emotional strength. Such moving masterpieces grip your heart with compassion, and at the same time you are heartened by the expressions of serenity in the face of hardship. In his *Buona Terra* series, Giacomelli also gives witness to the miraculous

change of seasons as a backdrop for the inside and outside of his subjects' daily lives via wheat harvests, grape pickings, and the observance
of ceremonies. You feel reassured that life marches on, and, although the
changes of season may bring new challenges, there will also be new joys.

People who adapt best to adversity are those who know how to periodically distance themselves from that adversity before it has a chance
to overwhelm them. Intentional distancing is not about denial or repres-
sion of your feelings. It is about developing the capacity to avoid getting
so swallowed up by grief that it defines your life. Hard work is a natural
remedy for negative feelings. It is also the perfect "distancer."

Work is already a major part of most people's lives. According to psychologists, it can also be a main source of personal satisfaction.[1] Not
everyone has to put in long days of physical labor in the fields like the
subjects in Giacomelli's photos do, or as my family does today in the
farmlands of Castelpagano. Whether you have an office job, volunteer
work, housework, a yard to clean up, a car to wash, or a roof that needs
repair, any type of work will help you press the "reset" button on your
trauma if you throw yourself into it and find a way to love doing it to
the best of your ability. Psychologist Abraham Maslow wrote that self-
esteem and the esteem of others are extremely important to feeling ful-
filled.[2] Both esteem categories can be derived from working to the best
of your ability.

How many times have you heard people say "I hate my job! I only do
it to get a paycheck at the end of the week"? Not everyone is passionate about his or her formal job, but to get over loss, your job can serve
as an excellent tool. No matter what kind of work you do or how little
you like it, forget about all of that right now. Instead, feed your mind
with all the positives about your job (it allows you to pay the bills, gives

you an opportunity to shine, gives you a sense of accomplishment when you complete a task well), and delve into your work with 100 percent absorption; you will begin to feel a transformation. Whether you go to work at the office or you are working from home, just imagine you are becoming one with your tasks, and think of nothing else but doing each task to the very best of your ability. Don't allow yourself to complain to yourself or to others. Let work help you feel better about yourself and pull you out of the stagnant state of melancholy that often follows loss.

Italians believe that hard work begets a happy life. My paternal relatives work hard with their hands and bodies from sunrise to sunset in Italy. The fruits of their labor allow them to eat and earn a living, but their work is also a remedy for emotional distress as much as it is a prescription for a limber body. My Italian loved ones are well up in age, and yet they are as spry as any young adult.

Roman Emperor Marco Aurelio wrote this in his book of *Meditations*:

> If thou workest at that which is before thee, following right reason seriously, vigorously, calmly, without allowing anything else to distract thee . . . expecting nothing, fearing nothing, but satisfied with the present activity . . . thou wilt live happy. And there is no man who is able to prevent this.[3]

Those are powerful words. It doesn't matter what kind of work you do. As long as you immerse yourself in the process, you will find relief from your heartache. Let your work be a vehicle for putting that planned "distance" between you and your troubles, even if only for brief intervals initially. Working in full-focus mode will distance you from your troubles. Whether the work is physical, creative, or intellectual, just apply yourself fully, and notice the positive feeling of satisfaction.

If possible, vary the kinds of work that you put your time into. If you work at a desk all day or work at intellectual tasks like teaching or writing, do some physical tasks when you come home. A *zia* (aunt) once told me that too much mind activity is *male* (bad); it throws us off balance. She was right. The sweat and toil of manual labor can bring satisfaction, whether that labor is from sowing a row of wheat, milking a cow, or giving your garden fence a fresh coat of white paint.

The Italian philosophy of *l'arte di arrangiarsi* (the art of getting by) lies partly in the ability to immerse oneself in hard work when times get tough. In many Italian villages, physical work is also commonly used as a way to stay focused on the task instead of on the negativity (fear, sadness, anxiety) that accompanies loss. Hard work can be a natural negative emotion corrector—no chemicals required. Michelangelo was not a farmer, but he was no stranger to letting distressing thoughts work themselves out in the course of engaging in hard work. Florence was under the threat of siege by rival states in his time, and he feared for his beloved city. So Michelangelo used his body and hands to create a solution. He locked himself in a workshop behind a cathedral and labored for three long years, practically nonstop, hammering and chiseling at a towering block of damaged marble. This marble would ultimately become the statue of David—a biblical hero symbolizing inner strength, a reminder to his fellow Florentines to find their own courage.

Balancing mental and physical work makes for a resilient mind that has no time to "ruminate." Throw yourself into work to *mollare i problemi* (let go of problems), at least long enough to encourage a new perspective to emerge. Life is about survival. Personal productivity through good hard work will restore your "can-do" confidence and your spirit.

Zia never had the opportunity for school-book knowledge, but she did have a rich, commonsense wisdom learned from working the land. "The problem with staying in your head all the time," *Zia* told me, "is that your problems just keep spinning. There is no peace. Work is different. There is a beginning. There is an end. *Basta* (Enough)."

Zia was a bulwark of confidence. She never second-guessed herself. I worked alongside her cleaning out the animal stalls, wondering, "Why on earth is she singing to the rhythm of milk squirting into a steel bucket at her feet?" A holy euphoria would come over the Italians in my family when they worked. I now know why. Work leaves no time for worry, and at the end of the day you have accomplished something that makes you aware of your own capabilities.

When I was younger, despite pressure from my father to do well in school, he would also be irritated when I spent long hours at the table doing homework. I didn't understand it then, but I do now. He was raised with the philosophy that sitting around weakens the body and the mind. It is true that if we sit around most of the time, eventually such a lifestyle will make us sick. How many of us stay in a sedentary position for hours in front of a computer before we get up to move around? Usually we can feel the effects on our bodies when we're stationary too long, but most of us don't make the connection between physical inertia and emotional stagnation.

In the past, there was plenty of opportunity for physical work. Many of us don't have these responsibilities today. Or if we do, we delegate work to others, such as landscapers who cut our grass, or the teenage boy down the street who wants to earn a few bucks cleaning out garages. Even when we decide to do the work ourselves, we often take short-cuts, which defeat the purpose: we buy the robotic vacuum that sucks up crumbs while we sit on the couch making more, or the 6-cylinder lawnmower that rides like a Mercedes and feels like a Henredon arm-chair. Depriving ourselves of physical work leaves us with lots of time for anxiety, worry, sadness—and all those unsettling states of mind end up being placated with an oversized cinnamon bun. Physical work is as much about emotional serenity as it is about physical fitness. Strive for a balance of physical and mental activities, and do both to the best of your ability.

Use Physical Work to Overcome Hard Times

If you want to use physical work to distance yourself from grief, make a list of tasks that work your body more than your mind. You can start by selecting one of the ideas below. Follow through three times a week, or even once a day if your full-time job is particularly sedentary. Once you get into the habit of balancing mental work with physical, you will begin to notice a wonderful change in your outlook. It is all about easing yourself forward into simpler times that foster self-pride and emotional adaptivity.

Fare il pane (**Make some bread**). In Italy, even food preparation gets physical. I remember having the best time helping my friend Mariana bake bread in her kitchen. We lugged big sacks of flour from the pantry and measured some into a large steel mixing bowl. Then we rolled up our sleeves and threw our weight into our knuckles until all the ingredients were mixed. Finally we pulled the dough onto the floured counter for some kneading and folding until it was time to let it rest. The end result was magnificent, but the process was even more so.

Consider buying a good bread recipe book. Put your bread maker away and commit to doing every step by hand, and to make it even more fun, have a friend or two over to join in the catharsis. That evening you can plan a delicious supper with the fruit of your efforts!

Accudire la casa (**Maintain your home**). Here, focus on the larger chores—mowing the lawn, trimming the hedges, sweeping the driveway, or washing and waxing the floors by hand. Do these tasks with focused concentration, to experience the pleasure of *fare* (doing).

Tendere al giardino (**Tend to your garden**). Italians tend to their gardens as they do their children—with love and dedication. As the proverb goes, *Chi non semina non raccoglie* (If you don't sow, you don't reap). Italians take that literally when it comes to gardening, but what they reap is far greater than *zucchine* and tomatoes. They reap the gratification of feeling the soil: smelling ripening grapes, the first green sprouts in spring—and a calm contented mind. Choose this option during gardening season, either by designating a modest space in your backyard or by using large pots if you don't have land. Make sure you tend to your garden lovingly, and lose yourself in every related action.

Costruire qualcosa (**Build something**). Italians don't run to hardware store experts every time they want to build something. They use their hands and bodies, just like their predecessors who built the aqueducts and the cobblestone roads that are made of several layers of different types of sand, mortar, gravel, and clay—each carefully positioned for durability and flexibility. It doesn't matter if you've never built anything before, you can start small—a small box for jewelry, a stone pathway in the yard. The only criteria are that it must involve physical movement and have your full mental involvement.

Fare servizio per gli altri (**Do a service for others**). Italians thrive when they can be of service to others. Renowned Sicilian-born medical doctor Luigi di Bella, for example, lived a life of service well into his eighties. He worked arduously, day and night and during holidays, in a race to find a vitamin-based treatment for cancer. He also worked as a professor, and, if any of his students missed class, he would accommodate their schedules, even if it meant cutting back on his own free time. Dr. di Bella received people at all hours of the day and night who made a pilgrimage to his home after traditional cancer treatments had failed them; some he claimed to have saved, others he lost. He persevered tirelessly and selflessly despite public criticism from his peers and the Italian government, who accused him of promoting an unscientific cure. Because he strongly believed in his ability to help others, he persevered, despite the obstacles he had to overcome.

Take a dog for a walk or run. Volunteer for regular dog walking at your local shelter, and you will feel great about getting the animals out of those cages to experience the sun, fresh air, and the outside world. Walk fast or jog, to get the body going and give one of God's amazing furry creatures a bright spot in their day.

Make pasta by hand. Look on the Internet or in your favorite Italian recipe book and you will find a recipe for homemade *cavatelli,* which are perhaps the easiest pasta to make by hand. Throw yourself into the dough making, rolling, and the shaping. You will get to enjoy your efforts as you replenish your energy with the final product.

Get more involved with your day job. Stay focused on your responsibilities, take them slowly—not in a frenzy—and don't give in to letting your mind wander back to upsetting thoughts. Remember, this is your intentional distancing time, a time for you to look at your job—or your additional physical labor activities—as a respite from your troubles. Begin right now with the physical task of making my recipe for *Scarola e Fagioli.* There is plenty of physical work in the washing, slicing, and chopping, with a physical benefit in the end when you get to eat these healthful ingredients. Let yourself become one with the preparation and cooking and you will find that your cares have disappeared.

Scarola e Fagioli (Escarole and Beans)

MAKES APPROXIMATELY 4 SERVINGS

2 to 3 tablespoons olive oil

1 large onion, chopped

½ pound pancetta (Italian bacon), chopped

Red crushed pepper flakes to taste

5 ripe tomatoes chopped, or ½ large can (28 ounces) plum
  tomatoes, chopped

1 or 2 heads green escarole, washed thoroughly and chopped

1 cup white beans, soaked overnight and then boiled until soft for 1 hour,
  or 1 (16-ounce) can white cannelloni beans, drained and rinsed.

1 teaspoon dried oregano

Salt and pepper to taste

Coat the bottom of a large saucepan with the olive oil and heat over medium heat until a drop of water placed in the pan sizzles. Add the onion, bacon, and red pepper flakes. Cook until the bacon is well browned. Add the tomatoes and the chopped escarole. Lower the heat and cook for ½ hour, stirring frequently. When the greens are nice and tender, add cooked or canned white beans and spices. Simmer five minutes to let the flavors combine. Enjoy with a nice crusty loaf of Italian bread.

15

Da Frequentare Spesso!:
Choose a Hangout and
Become a Regular

We are all fundamentally on our own . . . facing [one's]
solitude is a needed step on the way to recognizing [our]
essential solidarity with other beings.
—Piero Ferrucci, *What We May Be*

FOR ROMAN ORATOR MARCUS TULLIUS CICERO (106–43 BC), throwing himself into his writing after the death of his daughter Tullia was, as he put it, "the only way I can get away from my misery."[1] In fact, his literary output in the years following Tullia's death was more brilliant and copious than at any other time in his life.

The Loneliness of Loss

A gripping sadness pervades the great Giacomo Leopardi's *Il Passero Solitario* (*The Lonely Sparrow*). Leopardi (1798–1837) is one of Italy's most important historic treasures. This philosopher and poet created an extraordinary masterpiece of verbal art in describing the bittersweet similarity between his observations of the sparrow, for whom living a solitary life is instinctual, and his own life, which became painfully solitary through the loss of his health and his youth. The sparrow could continue to be happy, because it had no capacity to dwell on its aloneness. Leopardi, having an exquisite mind for reflection, could not help but dwell on the sorrow he felt as his illness distanced him from nature and the world around him.[2]

A pervasive feeling of loneliness often accompanies a major loss. In Leopardi's case, the sicker he became, the lonelier he felt. Often when you are dealing with a personal crisis, you feel others no longer understand you. You feel marginalized, on the outside. How could others relate, after all, if they haven't walked in your shoes? The truth is, even if people tell you they have gone through "exactly the same situation," they really haven't, because they are not *you*. They may have gone through a similar situation, but no one has the uniqueness of your life. No two lives are ever identical. Psychologist Carl Rogers distinguished between sympathy and empathy: sympathy is recalling your own situations when trying to understand what someone else is going through; empathy is trying to put yourself in their shoes without comparing it to what you went through.[3] Most people sympathize. Empathy, however, is the only way to communicate real depth of understanding.

Recalling your own experiences as a foundation to relate to what someone else is going through is a natural reaction. When I was out to dinner with a few friends the other night, each was anxious to share their story of loss with me. One woman was still getting over the loss of her pet, another was having trouble adjusting to her new job. A third friend just found out she had diabetes and was mourning the loss of her previous seemingly perfect health. When others talk about *their* experiences when we are hurting and in need of comfort, we can feel even more isolated. Martin, for instance, had just received his layoff notice when the company began to fold. He had three young children to support, and in this economy he was right to be concerned about the difficult road ahead in finding another job. One afternoon, shortly before the layoff went into effect, a coworker stopped by Martin's office to see how he was doing. Martin broke down with emotion as he talked about how he might have to tell his wife and children that they would have to put their home up for sale and find a less expensive rental. Martin's friend told him to keep his chin up. He said the "same thing" had happened to him ten years ago and everything worked out fine in the end. With that, he left Martin's office and told Martin that if he ever needed to talk again, just buzz his extension line and he'd pay another visit.

While it might be encouraging to hear about how someone else pulled through a similar situation, the circumstances that Martin was facing in a much tougher economy than his friend had faced only made him feel like the seriousness of his predicament was being discounted. Martin's friend really didn't understand Martin's situation at all. This friend never had three children to support. He never had to tell his family they would have to leave their home. The friend presumed that Martin's path was identical to his, and, if he was able to "buck up and pull through it," so could Martin. While his intentions were good, the effect of this pep talk made Martin feel even more alone.

Loss disrupts our former sense of normalcy. You know you are not the same as you were before. Perhaps you see things from a different perspective now. Some of the old parts of your life no longer seem important. Some of the friends you used to like to hang out with don't seem to be able to relate to you anymore because they see you as having changed. And you have. Your life is more urgent. You may feel like you are watching life go by from outside the arena. After my mother died, all I saw when I went out were daughters and mothers shopping, laughing, having lunch together. It seemed like the world was full of these wonderful mother-daughter bonds but there would be no possibility of that anymore for me. When my husband died, I noticed other couples of our age and older holding hands the way we used to, the way we still "should" be, sharing adventures or simply being there in a concert hall seated next to each other. It was as if the world continued to spin, but I had stepped off the carousel, and, instead of participating, I had become an outside observer.

Living like you are on the outside looking in creates a solitary feeling. The reflective time you need to process your hardship can be isolating. There is no doubt that you need to stop or at least slow your pace after loss. There is also no doubt that you need time to ponder how to get back in the game and make a unique contribution that only you can make to the world. The traditional Italian lifestyle philosophy is about balance, however. *Non esagerare*: nothing to excess. At a certain point, you must also give yourself a push to get up and take action.

The old rules you used to live by may no longer apply. There are "lessons" and "gifts" in all of our experiences. They can help us to become whole again if we let them. Take action against isolation and resolve to make your life better each day.

Lessons of the Volcano

Despite Mother Nature's violent wrath, the 2012 eruption of Sicily's Mt. Etna was also a brilliant golden light show, spitting its magnificence high into the air and commanding reverence and attention from everyone and everything surrounding it. A volcanic eruption disrupts or destroys everything around it. All life in its proximity is burned out by molten ash. The air fills with gasses that bring about acid rain and carry tiny rock particles to areas well beyond the volcanic space. This can cause breathing difficulties, and worse. The hot lava wipes out plants, trees, animals, and people in its way. The water as well as the land is affected. When the action stops there is no more lightshow, no more beauty in the sky—only a ghostly trail of death in its wake.

But wait. The volcanic ash that now covers a barren land will eventually release nutrient-rich particles into the soil and create the optimal environment for lush young growth. Soon, a beautiful new terrain has sprung from what looked like completely dead earth. Consider your life this way after loss: Notice the first delightful moment that fills your once "deadened" heart with gladness. Notice the second, and then the third shoot of hope spring up: some good news, a new opportunity, a delightful invitation out of nowhere. Yes, life after loss will again be fertile and vibrant and exquisite. All of nature is equipped with a built-in resiliency. And that includes me and you.

The Phenomenon of Campanilismo

An important part of your post-loss personal renewal plan should be the reestablishment of your social life to put a stop to loneliness (which is different from productive alone time). The quality of our relationships affects the quality of our life, and the length of our life. The importance of a network of people who care—even if they say the wrong things now and then—cannot be underestimated.

Relationships are essential in the Italian culture. Italians revel in the close-knit ties of immediate and extended family, neighbors who show up at your door to bring you a hunk of their best cheese, and those familiar faces seen occasionally at church, at the coffee bar, or at the Italian Red Cross chapter one volunteers for every month. This network becomes the fabric that sustains us, even when a few threads become temporarily unraveled. The Italian concept of *campanilismo*, the tendency to form tight-knit communities, comes from the word *campanile*, or church bell. It refers to people's devotion to their community, neighborhood, or town. Community consists of the close-knit lives of people who feel a sense of love and belonging in the place they call home.

Recently I gave a keynote address to a small crowd of 100 people at an Italian-American organization. I told eager listeners how they could achieve their full potential by tapping into the wisdom of their heritage. A large part of our heritage emphasizes what psychologist Abraham Maslow stressed as the importance of love and belonging. Humans need social connections to have a sense of well-being.[4] I looked around the room that night and realized that I was seeing *campanalismo* in action. At the gathering were people of all walks of life coming together, united by the same passion for their heritage and their common mission for doing good for others in the community. Everyone was accepting, no matter what each one's individual circumstances were, and it was obvious that everyone felt a sense of belonging and brother/sisterhood through common membership in this organization.

When you allow loss to turn you into a victim, it is easy to feel like you are watching that lone sparrow that Leopardi observed. Eventually you will get back into some of your old routines—like going to work, coming home, eating supper, watching TV, and going to bed. But the comfort of routine alone can never substitute for a meaningful social life, which can offer you moral support and a sense of belonging. In short, we need other people in our life. We all share a common human bond, even though the details of our experiences differ. We also goof up once in a while. The Italian culture is a forgiving one, but there is also a cultural self-esteem that enables Italians to draw healthy boundaries.

Don't get too offended when others say careless things now and then if in general they add richness to your life. If you want to have relationships, you must be willing to let individuals be who they are and not expect them to be who you are, nor to read your mind when you need something from them. This doesn't mean you should disrespect yourself by submitting to negative relationships that are not worth salvaging, but you need to be tolerant of those whose heart is in the right place. You'll find it is worth it when you make a greater effort to get out and make new connections.

Building Community Takes Time

Loneliness can creep up suddenly and unexpectedly after loss. You think you are doing okay when you are alone, then suddenly a voice in your head tells you that you are not alone by choice, and you panic, fearing you may end up alone in life whether you like it or not.

Two years after her divorce, Joan had the good fortune to meet someone she really cared about again. In fact the two hit it off so well that the upset from her divorce seemed to vanish as she opened her heart up again to love Jerry. They became inseparable for the next year and a half, but little red flags kept cropping up, which in retrospect were signs that the relationship was in trouble. To assuage her loneliness, Joan ignored her instinct to break off the relationship, even though in her heart she knew it wasn't going to work. Why? She was afraid of being lonely.

While most of us long for true love and companionship, you can counter your loneliness in the meantime by building a sense of community, the way Italians do. The rest will iron itself out if you gravitate toward what really does foster your well-being and don't ignore what you really need to be happy.

Unfortunately, community just doesn't show up at your doorstep, especially if you don't live near a city. To my family outside of Benevento, community life is a priority, and they orchestrate gatherings of one type or another every day. It is up to *you* to build your own sense of community and make yourself be a part of it. You can do this by selecting places to frequent where "everybody knows your name." It could be a bookshop coffee nook, a local Italian import shop, an outdoor café, a library lecture series, or an evening of wine tasting at the local vineyard. Community is just a group of people who share common interests or goals; it's where people keep an eye out for each other's safety, where they gather together to share ideas, laughter, and good food, and where people sustain you and you do the same for them. The only common denominator needed is a willingness to become a part of something greater than yourself.

Ways to Build a Sense of Community

✓ **Special interest groups** are listed online and in the newspaper. Don't feel like you have to stick to a group if it doesn't click, but now is the time to strengthen your adventure muscle, even if you are not used to going out alone or trying new things. If you like to write, there are local chapters of national writers organizations, as well as book stores and libraries that run writers groups. If you like spirituality, there are a number of spiritual groups, all designed with a common theme. If you like to cook, get out there and join a cooking class for an exotic ethnic cuisine you never would have thought about learning before. Open up your world, and community will blossom around you.

✓ **Adult education classes** have wide offerings. Try something completely new or get even better at a skill you need more practice in. Everything from computers to target shooting to cooking Italian food is offered at extremely reasonable prices.

✓ **Take a dance class.** You don't have to go for the expensive chains that pressure you into months and months of lessons at high fees. The last thing you need right now is to drain your wallet and worry about finances. Instead, there is a whole dance community near you that may require a little asking around but most are really low-key and fun. These are held at community and civic associations. The show *Dancing with the Stars* has made affordable dance lessons even more popular and you may make some lasting friends through this common interest.

✓ **Your place of worship** can be an ideal venue for building community in your neighborhood. You can often become part of some really great projects that help others. Feeling valued is like a soothing balm for a heart in distress. Get active and give yourself this healing experience.

✓ **Build your own community** by starting a community watch, a block tag sale, or a block-party barbecue, and get some of your neighbors or family members to help out with the set up.

✓ **Have a potluck supper.** You shouldn't have to worry about shopping, cooking, and cleaning up when it is really you who needs the care. Instead, invite a few acquaintances who you would like to get to know better. Tell them you're organizing a potluck with the sole purpose of getting to know each other better, and tell them also exactly what to bring so the meal is well balanced. All you have to do is buy disposable paper products, and you can avoid the clean up, too.

✓ **Family reunions.** At our family reunion in Castelpagano various relatives got together and shared duties in the kitchen. It was a massive, joyful, and bustling party. Seventy relatives filled the house. We sat on folding chairs and used makeshift tables. The important thing was being together to exchange stories, share photos, capture memories, commiserate with one another's aches and pains, and create a new memory that would last forever.

✓ **Go online.** One popular online event calendar is *Meetup*, where you can find interest groups showcased by area on http://meetup .com. If you don't find an event in your area that you want to join, then start one yourself! It is not a big investment, and you could collect dues to cover the cost of the subscription.

✓ **Book club or language club.** If you enjoy a certain genre of book, put an ad in the paper to meet other like-minded readers at a public coffee house. You might want to tell the owner ahead of time so they know what kind of turnout to expect based on the number of responses you have received. They win too, as everyone buys at least a beverage and often a snack to go along with it. You can start a language club the same way. Several years ago I spotted a tiny ad in a local paper for an Italian conversation group. A few of the friendships I made there will last as long as I do and have certainly lasted long after Saturday morning attendance became impossible for me. You can limit your book or language discussions to an hour and then keep to that time limit so everyone knows what to expect.

✓ **Become a regular at a coffee bar.** Choose one that looks interesting, and frequent it at the same time of day, most days of the week. Sit down and enjoy your cup of coffee as you read the newspaper or a magazine. Notice the people around you and reach out to make small talk, even if just a phrase or two. You can make someone else's day as well as your own. Detach from your mobile devices and make live, personal connections. Get to know the name of your server or waitperson, and little by little you will have built a bit of that *Cheers* feeling, "a place where everybody knows your name," and where they even begin to miss you when you don't show up on your regular day.

When you see how easy it is to build a community, you will wonder why you didn't take decisive steps to connect to others sooner. It is time to take action in all-important areas of your life if you really want to turn your loss into your personal renaissance. Renew your life with all the tools you have available to you. Come out of the dark ages of sadness. Don't underestimate the power you have to coax fresh green shoots from beneath what looks like nothing but the barren ash of a once-mighty volcano of crisis. Even mighty crises settle down eventually and give way to a stunning new scenario. Balance periods of needed solitary time with needed social time, and get back your passion for life!

Parte Quarta (Part IV)

Andare Avanti!: Time to Move Forward (and into Your Renaissance)!

16

Buona Salute:
Good Health, Italian Style

A tavola non si invecchia.

At the table, one never grows old.

—Italian proverb

A TUSCAN PROVERB GOES LIKE THIS: *Chi vuol viver sanamente, viva sobrio e allegramente* (If you want to be healthy, live sober and happily). Extremes can lead to problems. Some people cannot eat a thing when they are afflicted by crisis; others eat in a crazed frenzy, hoping that the next bite will be the one that dulls their emotional suffering. Both are self-destructive, self-neglectful habits, and both must be stopped before your health begins to decline. The same goes with exercise, which is usually the first thing to go out the window at a time when you most need the strength that comes from regular physical activity. While you may not feel you have the energy to devote to your health, this is one time when you have to just trudge through it until it becomes automatic. Take action and get back on track to putting your emotional and physical wellness before anything else. Make it a top priority to be strong, vibrant, and happy again.

The Italian Passion for Food

Turning fresh, locally produced foods into traditional reminders of who we are makes mealtime in Italy a therapeutic experience for both body and mind. A Mediterranean lifestyle is the solution to health risks caused by poor alimentary habits and physical inactivity. Equally important are the social and emotional aspects derived from Italian mealtime.

Marcello Barducci, proprietor of the beautiful Casale di Brolio in Tuscany, describes the Italian passion for food this way:

> My passion for food comes from the fact that the materials used in cooking are tied to the traditions of the people, to their lives, to their way of working. Local foods come from the same territories in which the people live, and they are linked to their culinary traditions. In other words, food, the way that it is eaten and cooked, is an expression of ourselves and of our lives. I believe it is very important to discover and maintain these ties to our past. Following a line that brings us from a recipe to the ingredients contained therein, to the various techniques of cooking these recipes, through food we discover so many things about ourselves and about our people.[1]

Eating healthfully is one of the most important things you can do to maintain good health following personal trauma. There is no shortage of research on the disease-fighting benefits of the Mediterranean diet.

It is a holistic experience that begins with a daily stop at a local market or town square's produce stand. The conversation, the decision making, the information gathering all give you a sense that you are part of a community. You come home with your ingredients and begin to create the sounds of life: rinsing, chopping, sizzling, and simmering. You are now putting your energy into good self-care. Cooking from old family recipes can even make you feel closer to the family members who made those dishes from generations past. An Italian approach to eating well can optimize your health, and give you the motivation to keep going and keep loving life.

My Italian ancestors never questioned their crises. They accepted that much in life is beyond our control. That was the real key to their serenity. Coming together for mealtime was our anchor, our nurturing rhythm, our reassuring and reliable routine. Mealtime was where everyone came to feel better from outside and inside troubles.

Each of our earthly journeys is unique. Our peaks and valleys come at different times and have different depths and intensities. The traditional Italian table experience provides nutrition to give you strength, company to make you feel supported, and laughter to remind you that life goes on and so does joy.

Non Esagerare: Don't Exaggerate!

La Lega Italiana per la Lotta contro i Tumori (The Italian League for the Fight Against Tumors) found that 65 percent of tumors are caused by either poor eating habits (35 percent) or smoking (30 percent). In other words, many cancers are caused by lifestyle habits that *we can change*. In addition to giving up smoking, the most important change we can make is the way we feed ourselves and how much physical activity we give to our bodies. Fad diets and pharmaceuticals for weight loss are denounced by the Italian Ministry of Health, which decries them as "big business with little scientific research behind them."[2] When you think about it, all we really need to do to have good eating habits is eliminate three things: junk foods, hurried eating, and excess. There is no magic to making sensible choices. You don't need sprinkles, pills, or magic potions. You need massive focus and actions to change your eating habits now. The same is true for exercise, the other major influence on good health.

Italians subsume physical activity into their overall daily lifestyle. Moving and keeping active is a natural part of Italian life. A good example is the homes along the Amalfi Coast. These are built right into the side of the mountain, leaving their inhabitants—young and old—no choice but to take multiple trips up and down stair paths each day. In the Naples region, Italian grade-school children participate in a program called *ortogym* (garden gymnastics). They tend a vegetable garden for one hour a day as part of Italy's contemporary solutions to prevent obesity and its related diseases.

In general, the traditional Italian prescription for staying active is not the gym, but rather gardening, daily walks, bike rides to the market in place of car rides, or taking the renowned after-dinner *passeggiata* (stroll). Working out like crazy for forty-five minutes and then spending the rest of the day seated in front of a computer or in your car makes little sense and makes no impact on your fitness over the long run. Italians believe that excess in anything is counterproductive. *Non esagerare* (don't exaggerate) is a common Italian refrain.

Be Proactive About Eating and Staying Active

When trauma disrupts your life, you hardly have the energy to think about sticking to any regime for eating and exercising. The most important thing immediately following your crisis is to get your bearings and start to process what is happening to you. If you let your life stay inert for too long, however, you may comprise good health habits and start a cycle of harmful routines. Before long, letting yourself go can cause you to lose ground and gain weight, which will make you even more distressed, which will diminish the motivation to reverse the damage.

Consider a *bel paese* (beautiful Italy) approach to exercising that feels natural and joyful, such as bicycling, hiking, walking, gardening, swimming, doing house- or yard work. Let natural activity become the solid foundation upon which you build this brand-new phase of the life you will now celebrate.

The town of Campodimele (mentioned in Chapter 7) is one of the few agricultural villages in Italy that is still self-sustaining. It is referred to as the town of longevity, and a lot has been written about this. When I asked the owner of Campodimele's only small hotel for his "secret" to the townspeople's long life, he did not hesitate. "We grow our own food, we don't stress over the things people in the larger cities stress over, we go to bed at sunset and get up at sunrise, and in between the two we work hard and have fun together, too."

What could be a simpler recipe for good health?

Benefits of a Mediterranean Lifestyle

The Mediterranean diet wins hands down for the prevention of diseases such as obesity, cardiovascular disease, high blood pressure, diabetes, and cancer, especially when compared to the standard American diet (SAD). In the 1950s, researcher Ancel Keys and his colleagues launched a major groundbreaking longitudinal study across seven countries. His findings revealed the disease-fighting properties of following a Mediterranean way of eating such as the one found in Southern Italy.[3] Proponents of the Mediterranean diet recommend your meals consist mostly of fruits and vegetables, whole grains, nuts, beans, legumes, and seeds for a healthy supply of antioxidants; use a good brand of extra-virgin olive oil in moderation and in place of butter and other fats, incorporate some fish for omega-3 fatty acids, use tomatoes for lycopene, and if you eat animal protein you should do so sparingly. Poultry can be consumed two to three times a week, lean red meat only once or twice a month, and a small amount of dairy occasionally. Sweets are to be used only very occasionally. Red wine and coffee can be used in moderation, perhaps a glass of wine with evening meals and maybe a couple of cups of a good espresso coffee per day. The Mediterranean diet lifestyle also includes lots of activity throughout the day. Your body can't digest food correctly if you are overly sedentary.

A Mediterranean lifestyle plan also improves body image. Generally speaking, when you follow this way of eating and stay active, you won't have to be overly concerned about your body weight. It will normalize on its own. My own research found less of a discrepancy between the actual and ideal body image for Italians than for either Americans or the British. Body mass index (BMI) is in fact lower on average for

Italians than for the other two cultures; this also increases Italians' self-confidence when it comes to being satisfied with the way they look.[4] When you are going through loss, don't allow sadness to ravage your body. You can use the Mediterranean approach to guard against this. It is a celebration of life, which is exactly what is called for. No one is talking about perfection. As a culture, while Italians stay fit to feel their best, they are very forgiving when it comes to a few extra pounds. A recent survey showed that more than 80 percent of Italian men found curves and a bit of padding to be much more attractive than excessive skinniness.[5]

A Mediterranean diet may even reduce cognitive deficits and dementia. I know that most people who are going through loss report a kind of a brain drain. Their thoughts become muddled, and they feel confused and depressed. Switching to a Mediterranean diet may help you stay clearheaded and focused.[6] The Italian Society of Gerontologists and Geriatrics (Società Italiana di Gerontologia e Geriatria [SIGG]) reports that the antioxidants and polyphenols found in a Mediterranian diet are related to lower occurences of Alzheimer's disease and other types of dementia. The health-promoting elements of wine, olive oil, coffee, and nuts (all in moderation) seem to keep the brain young.

The Mediterranean Switch

Mari lost her job and became addicted to sweets. Her friends initially showed support by bringing cakes and cookies. Soon Mari was starting her day with donuts, grabbed some sweetened cereal for lunch, and worked her way through an entire fruit pie for supper, justifying this by saying that she was at least getting her fruit requirement for the day.

When I saw Mari after some time had gone by, she looked as if she had aged considerably.

Stress and anxiety, together with an extra few pounds, have a way of rapidly aging the outer appearance, but they also damage the inside of your body. The right eating habits can counteract frazzled emotions and reverse cravings and food addictions.

If you have been letting emotional or reactive eating habits rule your lifestyle, resolve to make the switch today. Start feeding your body with the nutrients it needs and deserves as an act of self-love. There is no one else who can do this for you. Make a pledge to nurture yourself and give your body back its lifeline. Give yourself what your body needs to resist disease and debilitation with the simplicity of the Southern Italian eating and lifestyle habits found to be so protective against disease.

Consider this to be the start of a renewed commitment to your health and well-being. Write these statements down on note cards and put them where you will see them when you first wake up in the morning:

- ✓ I will feed my body only foods that promote good heath from this day forward. I will eat only the foods that my cells crave and not what my emotions think I should crave.
- ✓ I will shop locally grown foods, make simple Mediterranean meals, and enjoy mealtime with friends and family.
- ✓ I will not put my emotional and physical health at risk through a sedentary lifestyle and poor eating habits.
- ✓ I will walk, bike, garden, swim, hike, dance, clean, and experience the joy of movement each and every day.

Perform a brief meditation whenever you get a junk-food craving; it will keep you from using food to calm your anxiety, sadness, or stress.

You'll find several examples at http://raeleenmautner.com. You will find that your level of frenzy for eating automatically and without thinking will begin to calm down. Your cravings will begin to pass, and you will find yourself in a calmer zone where you can refocus on the business of living.

Your Healthy Mediterranean Kitchen

Healthy eating is best achieved through cooking, but the only way people stick with cooking is if they can make it fun. I like to create an ambience for cooking that makes me feel energized and not overworked. I play some beautiful music as background, invite a couple of friends to chop and peel along with me, and always start with fresh ingredients as a way to respect the gift of good health.

The basic guidelines for Mediterranean mealtimes are as follows:

Breakfast—a simple whole-grain roll with fresh fig marmalade, caffé latte, and a fruit.

Lunch—a simple dish of pasta or vegetable soup and a salad. You can even have a whole-grain panino with mozzarella, tomato, and basil with a drizzle of olive oil.

Dinner—a green salad, vegetables, and fish or a light meat such as roasted chicken.

Between meals—Italians love their coffee breaks, and sometimes they eat a piece of fruit as well. A handful of nuts is another healthy option for a snack.

Pantry Staples

You can't go wrong if you keep your pantry stocked with dried Italian herbs and spices (but see my caveat under Refrigerator Basics below). My "go-to" dried spices and herbs include oregano, parsley flakes, rosemary, basil, onion powder, garlic powder, and dried hot pepper flakes. How you combine these ingredients is limited only by your *fantasia* (imagination). Other pantry items I love to keep on hand include cans of San Marzano plum tomatoes, Italian crushed tomatoes, and tomato paste. For pastas I go for Barilla whole-grain basic shapes: elbows for soups and stews, spaghetti, and a tubular pasta such as ziti or rigatoni. I like to keep at least four cans of Genova *tonno* (tuna) packed in olive oil on hand. It can be used for a marvelous tuna sauce for pasta, or can be eaten right from the can with a ripe tomato salad to accompany it for lunch. A bag of mixed nuts in their shells with a piece of fresh fruit and some great cheese make a wonderful dessert.

Sugar is probably the most addicting substance you can eat. Avoid large amounts of it. Italian desserts like tiramisu are scrumptious, but you can make lighter versions when you prepare them yourself; and, even then, eat them sparingly and only occasionally to avoid cravings. Fig marmalade (made with the fruit and some of the skin) is often seen on the Italian breakfast table alongside some hot brioche and caffè latte. It is a lighter way to satisfy your sweet tooth. Besides fruit, Italian imported biscotti usually contain much less sugar than cookies sold here. I also encourage you to make your own biscotti and desserts, so you can control sugar content or substitute the sugar for other natural sweeteners.

Refrigerator Basics

Do shop for produce at your local community farmer's market when in season. Go organic whenever you can. Italians have an aversion to genetically modified anything and pesticides as well. Think rainbow colors to maximize the variety of fruits and vegetables you consume. Deep-purple eggplant; bright-green zucchini; colorful, juicy citrus fruits; purple plums; blueberries; red, green, and golden apples; and lots and lots of deep green leafies (dandelion, kale, broccolini, collards, escarole, and spinach). My father, who swears that greens are the secret to his good health, eats them almost every day in the form of a salad, soup, or mixed with pasta. He is ninety-two years young at this writing.

Also, remember to buy fresh parsley, basil, and tomatoes whenever you can. The pantry versions are to be used in a pinch. Those fresh herbs and tomatoes can go into tomato sauce, pesto, sandwiches of mozzarella, tomato, and basil with a drizzle of olive oil, or a quick pasta with beans, parsley, onion, and celery, with a side green salad. Southern Italian cuisine is simple, fun to make, and nutritious.

Putting It All Together

Italians are known for whipping up delicious, simple meals with whatever they have in the pantry and fridge. I am no exception. I approach cooking as a fun experience, not a chore. It allows me to be as creative as I wish while doing something great for myself and whomever else joins in.

I learned the joyful art of this style of cooking from my grandparents and parents. It served me well as I went through the crises in my life. Remember, your health is always worth your attention and time.

My grandmother cooked all kinds of simple "peasant food," as people call it today. *Pasta e patate* (pasta and potatoes) was one of my favorites. It is delicious, inexpensive, and easy to make. Here is how I cook *pasta e patate* when I need a healthy carb fix:

1. Play some great Italian songs.
2. Pour myself a glass of wine.
3. Scout the pantry and refrigerator to see what I have.
4. Put my dish together and call a couple of friends over to join me.

There are a hundred variations on any Italian dish you could possibly cook, so don't be afraid to experiment, and don't feel like you need each ingredient to make the recipe exact. Italians don't like rigidity, but very much prefer creativity. Here is my basic recipe:

Pasta e Patate

MAKES 4 TO 6 SERVINGS

2–3 tablespoons salt

10 cups water (enough to fill a large pot ¾ full)

½ pound elbow macaroni (I like the whole-grain variety that was used in the old days)

2–3 tablespoons olive oil

2 potatoes, finely diced

½ large onion, finely diced

1–2 stalks celery, chopped

2 tablespoons tomato paste

Splash of balsamic vinegar or red drinking wine

Red pepper flakes to taste (optional)

4 cups reserved pasta water

Fresh basil to taste, shredded finely (or any Italian
herb or spice, fresh or dried)

Grated Parmesan cheese

Add the salt to the water and bring to a boil in a large Dutch oven. Add the elbows and cook till al dente, according to the package directions. Drain and save 4 cups of the pasta water. Coat the bottom of a frying pan with olive oil. When the oil is hot, add the potatoes. Stir over medium heat, to make sure the potatoes don't burn. When the potatoes are starting to get soft (approximately 10–15 minutes), add the onion and celery and stir. Sauté all until the onions are translucent. Add the tomato paste, vinegar, dried spices, and the pasta water. Lower the heat and simmer for 20 minutes. Add the fresh basil right before removing from the heat. Combine the cooked pasta with the potato mixture. Top with the Parmesan cheese. Serve with a fresh arugula salad dressed with lemon juice and drizzled with olive oil.

Variation: You can also add cooked, crumbled pancetta to the dish if you like a bit of crunch and bacon flavor in your *pasta e patate.*

An Italian Mediterranean diet is not hard to follow, nor hard to prepare. But while you don't have to spend huge amounts of time in food preparation, you do have to devote some time to honoring yourself and your good health through cooking. Nutritious home-cooked meals help you fight disease and stay strong. You deserve it, so put the extra effort in and enjoy! *Buon appetito* (Eat well)!

17

Ogni Mattina: Let Every Morning Bring a New Day

In every product of earth there is an inborn power.
This is the power by which a minute fig-seed, or a
grape-stone, or the tiniest of seeds of any crop or root,
are transformed into vast trunks and branches.

—Marcus Tullius Cicero (106–43 BC)

ORNING ALWAYS BRINGS A NEW DAY, and you will recognize this when you least expect it. Suddenly you will become aware that you are smiling and laughing a lot more than you have in recent times. You are starting to look forward to the future and are really enjoying the present. You have put the sorrow of your crisis behind you and realize that life is still worth living. You know that as long as you are still breathing you will have what it takes to love, laugh, be of service to others, and truly enjoy being alive. You also know that you are now more capable than ever of getting through life's obstacles. Look how far you have already come!

Italians pride themselves on their ability to *arrangiarsi*, get through their difficulties and keep going forward. They are quick to recall the previous crises they have overcome. A few years ago a survey conducted by Demos-Coop showed that 60 percent of Italians predicted that Italy's financial crisis would continue with no end in sight.[1] Unemployment rates soared through the roof, more young adults than ever had to live at home with their parents, and personal savings—something Italians used to make a priority—were at an all-time low in attempts just to make ends meet. Yet when Italians were interviewed on the economic threat to their well-being, their reactions were not quite what most people would expect: "And so there's a crisis, what else is new?" one Italian commented. "It's not as if we are not used to hard times. In Italy, we know how to get along."

As reported in *La Repubblica,* what buffers most Italians from crisis is their strong sense of community, and confidence in the *arte d'arrangiarsi* (the belief in one's ability to get by), which we discussed in the Introduction. In psychological language, that *arte d'arrangiarsi* is called self-efficacy—the belief that you will succeed at specific tasks.[2] Confidence that you will succeed keeps motivation strong when your situation looks dismal. Italians never lose confidence in their ability to live a happy life, despite adversity. Believe in your ability to do the same.

Pino was one of the only ones from his town in Southern Italy to have the opportunity—at great sacrifice to his family—to go to university. He studied engineering and worked hard to make his family proud. Since he was a little boy he had been on a mission to help his family break free of poverty. Although they made do with what little they had,

Pino watched his mother and father go without things for themselves in order to send him to school; for example, his mother had only one dress for church and one for around the house in her closet. Her shoes had holes in them, so she inserted pieces of cardboard inside to keep her feet warm.

While Pino had no sense of missing out on anything, he had a keen sense of being the only possibility to help his family. Although his father could have really used his help to run the family grocery store, he was willing to go it alone if it meant Pino had the chance of pursuing a better life. Unfortunately, Italy had a high unemployment rate for college graduates and, even with a diploma in hand, Pino found it impossible to find a job. The Italian aging population and down economy has meant that Italians are not able to retire as early as they once did, and many are hanging on to the jobs that would otherwise have gone to young graduates.

Eventually Pino came back home with his head hung low and a heavy heart. He felt he had let his family down. That evening he sat at the table with his family and told them how discouraged he felt.

"Enough worrying," Pino's father said. "You'll see that morning will bring a brand-new day."

He turned out to be right. Pino was put in charge of the family grocery store and discovered how much he loved waiting on customers. He had to admit he very much enjoyed making small talk with the people in his town, and there was always a warm conversation at the ready. His customers loved him, too. Pino decided that he might try again for a job in the city the next year, but for now this was the brand-new morning that returned him to serenity and peace. He actually hated being in the big city with the noisy traffic and around people who were always in a hurry. He felt swallowed up by the high rises and the slick designer suits. What he really needed was to be right where his heart was, at least for now. He realized that happiness, not some fancy job, was what he really wanted for himself.

Isn't the ability to be happy the common denominator of all of our dreams?

We have all felt the sadness and disappointment of having to change or even abandon our goals. Pino got over his aspiration of being an engineer in the city pretty quickly. He had the support of his family and his neighbors. He had the little family business to go back to, and above all he believed in his ability to get by and survive no matter what happened from now on. He was fully aware that the family grocery store might not only be his present but might also very well be his destiny. Yet Pino welcomed that day as his new day, and his disappointment faded away.

Recipe for Un Giorno Nuovo *(A New Day)*

No matter what you have been through, your new day is at hand. Let today be the dawn of a new adventure, and no longer just another day to mourn your loss. Now you are in the *fare* (to-do zone). Remember how you've come through difficulties before, and you will get through them right now. Here are some ideas that might work for you:

- ✓ *Basta!* Enough! Say it aloud whenever you feel yourself backsliding into reliving your trauma. We all need to step out of gloom and heal our emotional wounds solidly and completely.
- ✓ Dream a new dream. Suggest ways for your friends and family to support you with your new dream. Pino's new dream was to be happy running the family store. His father has since passed away, and today the

store means more to him than any engineering job he could have been hired for. He is now one of the most admired figures in his local community. In the city, he may have been just one of thousands of new college graduates trying to make a living.

✓ Think of your life as one of Michelangelo's *non-finito* (unfinished) sculptures. A *non-finito* is a work purposely left unfinished to remind us that we are ever in a state of becoming. Your life is a masterpiece, which you will continually chisel as you go along.

✓ Free your mind of regrets, frustrations, and grief for most of the day. Express your feelings about your loss when you need to, but refuse to ruminate over it and keep rewounding your spirit. Make as much of your day as possible be about moving forward.

✓ Choose to be around people who give you peace and serenity. Don't go out with friends who make you feel anxious or who don't support what you are going through. It is better to stay home and watch a good movie than come home feeling defeated. Stay away from people you can't trust.

✓ Accept whatever reality you are living in now, and find a way to make it work. Whether you are newly living alone, or suddenly find yourself without a job, or in a new city where you don't know a soul, just stop for a moment and pause. Now think about some of the positive aspects of where you are now—think of anything positive at all. Use that as a starting point and then think of where you can go from here to rebuild a life you can love.

✓ Be your own best friend. Loving friends and family are crucial to Italians, but so is loving who you are. That is why the *bella figura* (putting your best foot forward at all times) is so important. Putting your best foot forward is a sign that you like yourself well enough to stand tall and with dignity. Don't wallow in grief or sorrow. Don't live in sweatpants, because although they may feel comfortable, they can eventually make you begin to feel miserable. Get up, get dressed, get going. Push yourself into your bright new day. You are about to turn your life around.

✓ Seek intellectual stimulation. Learn something new, engage in honest debate, go to a museum, or take a nighttime course—all will lead to new neural pathways that keep you evolving as you move forward. You never know if your new knowledge will lead to a new business, hobby, new friends, or further training for an eventual career update. Stay smart and keep learning. If you have recently lost a spouse, you are no doubt learning to do new things that once fell under the auspices of his or her traditional role. There is nothing to say that a woman cannot learn mechanics or that a man cannot learn to cook. Make a statement to yourself that your new learning will bring you to a new morning.

✓ Stay away from excess in anything. When people are beaten down by adversity they seek comfort from overshopping, overdrinking, overmedicating, promiscuity, and other exaggerations. *Non esagerare* (Don't exaggerate). Steer clear of extremes of anything. Stay safe, planted, and right in the middle. The last thing you need is to compromise your well-being. Today is about building you up.

✓ Stay flexible. Don't be afraid to change your mind if you feel like it. You may have promised a friend you would give her a ride but this morning you woke up with a head cold. This is a legitimate reason to change your mind. Strengthen your "no" muscle and use it when you need to keep from spreading yourself too thin.

✓ Stay aware of what life teaches you. In Pino's case, it taught him that no matter what his situation, he could find a way to be content. Everything that happens to you also offers you a way to move forward if you seek it.

✓ Finish the things you start. Leaving tasks incomplete is bad for your self-esteem. If you start to apply for a job and then put it aside because two letters of recommendation are required, make sure you follow through and get those letters, and then check that item off your list. This will give you a sense of accomplishment.

✓ Stay the course. You can either get swallowed up by your downtrodden state, or you can get up, persevere, and discipline yourself to get out of your victim rut and get back into the game. Until you breathe your last breath, there is something you can do to make your life happier. Do it. Figure out what happiness means to you, and pursue it. Would it mean more friends? Join a club or church. Would it mean having better relationships with your family members? Have a cookout and invite everyone over. Would it mean finding inner peace? Join a meditation or yoga class. Don't stop until you have met your happiness head on. Remember, there will always be moments when your grief comes back like a wave that rushes over you. It will do that all on its own. Your job is to be content in your other moments.

✓ Stop thoughts. If you have any ruminative or sad thoughts throughout the day—apart for the time you might set apart to reflect on your loss or adversity—you should stay right on the course toward happy thoughts. Imagine a large red stop sign whenever you start to think about sadness or negativity during the rest of your day, and then switch your thoughts by placing them deliberately on what is light, humorous, positive, life-affirming, motivating, empowering, heartening, or encouraging. Keep going, don't give up. As Italian parents will call to their soccer-star kids: "*Non arrenderti mai* (Never give up)!"

✓ Don't compare yourself to others. Social comparison theory says that when we make upward comparisons (such as *that person is better looking, has more money, more smarts,* or *is in a better position than I am*), we always end up feeling worse about ourselves. Every person is unique, every situation is unique; it makes no more sense to ask "Why me?" than it does to wonder "Why them?" Just focus on making your life the best it can be, and keep going. You are the architect of your own happiness. Build it to your own specifications right now.

✓ Make sure your words are kind, not bitter. When you are feeling slighted by the events that didn't go your way, it is easy to get embittered, and a subtle or not so subtle hostility or dryness comes out in the things you say and how you relate to other people. Beware. This way of relating will not evoke supportive feelings from others—quite the opposite. People will want to keep their distance from you and avoid talking to you about certain things because they are turned off by your reactions. When you relate to other people, remember that each one of us is going through a journey that has bumps placed at different junctures, but nevertheless adversity is something we all face and try our best to get through.

✓ Stop blaming yourself. You are put on this earth to learn, and, if you are doing so, you have no reason to blame yourself. Survivor's guilt is real, especially when someone we love passes away. Start now in making your relationships with others the way they should be. Apologize when you have offended, draw boundaries where you need to, keep those you love close by and those who cause you problems farther away. Do your best every day and you won't have reason to blame yourself for anything. We all make mistakes.

✓ Look at the tough parts of your life as challenges to be overcome. Motivate yourself to keep going. *If I can get through today, I will put a star on the page, and, when I have five stars in a row, I will buy myself a new scarf.* Yes, you might call it bribing yourself, but it works. Look at your challenges as doable bumps on the road so you don't fall into the inertia of defeat.

✓ Don't exceed your physical limits. You are human, not bionic. You need food, rest, sleep, exercise, and social interaction. Don't let yourself go without checking your requirements regularly. Don't ever ignore the principles of good health.

✓ Have fun every day. Do one thing each day that brings a smile to your face; that's all. It can last five minutes—like a good laugh with a friend—or it can last an hour, like the funniest movie you have ever seen. Do something though, anything, to add fun and enjoyment in your day.

The time has come to reinvent the story of your life. Time is a limited gift that you cannot afford to waste by staying miserable. Being alive is an honor and a privilege. You were given the gift of another new morning. Think of how you will use it, what you will do with it, and how to (unfinished) become your own *non-finito*. This day is for you. You are not here to just "tolerate" but to celebrate.

Buon giorno! Welcome to your new morning!

La Trasformazione:
Transform Yourself and
Your Life with a Makeover

Il processo di trasformazione dovrebbe avvenire sempre in noi.
Quotidianamente.
The process of transformation must always come from within us.
Daily.

—Valerio Albisetti, *Come Attraversare la Sofferenza*

N CHAPTER 7, I WROTE ABOUT THE IMPORTANCE of exposing yourself to external beauty on a daily basis. This chapter is about giving yourself a *bella figura* (putting your best foot forward) makeover inside and out. It will transform how you feel about yourself and how others react to you. In fact, a positive reaction to beauty appears to be hardwired in our brain. Researchers at the University of Parma showed volunteers an original image of the sculpture *Doryphoros* by Polykleitos, as well as several distorted versions. The original sculpture abides by the "golden mathematical rule of symmetry," considered to be the ideal of beauty by Renaissance artists. When participants viewed the original image, certain sets of their brain cells were activated—including the insula, which mediates emotion. Images thought of as beautiful also activated the brain's right amygdala, the part of the brain associated with emotionally laden memories.[1]

Dr. Piero Ferrucci, author of *Beauty and the Soul*, believes that beauty is physically and emotionally healing, inspiring, and stimulating. Ugliness, according to Ferrucci, has the opposite effect. It depresses us, upsets our inner world, and makes us feel weak and incapable.[2] So what is beauty, and how do we give ourselves an inner and outer beauty makeover?

In Italy there is a saying: *Non è bello ciò che è bello, ma è bello ciò che piace* (What is in itself beautiful is not beautiful; what is beautiful is what pleases you). Ferrucci believes that beauty is a way of being, and that it can change your life. I believe that it can also reverse the effects of the "ugliness" of the trauma you have just been through. In addition to beautifying your surroundings, tending to the various aspects of your personal beauty can also play an important role in restoring your zest for life. Let inner and outer beauty lend serenity and sweetness to your new personal renaissance.

Ferrucci discovered that beauty could literally transform a person into someone new: someone with a different character, a more intense love for life, and a richer inner and outer life manifested by greater confidence, self-esteem, and better relationships with other people.[3] The therapeutic benefits of beauty can lead you to a more satisfying existence and a feeling of increased happiness in this new phase of your life. Immersing yourself with the healing power of beauty involves sweetening the actions you take, the things you look at, listen to, smell, and surround yourself with. You can also give your body a simple Italian beauty makeover.

Put More Beauty into Your Actions

What would happen if instead of getting irritated with the slowness of the grocery check-out aisle, you took advantage of the opportunity to read a great magazine, or start a pleasant conversation with the person in back of you. Think how much more cheerful you will feel, in lieu of saying something nasty to show your irritation.

When is the last time you visited an art museum? Check out the exhibitions near you that reflect the kind of art you find beautiful, and treat yourself at least once a month to an unhurried afternoon of art/beauty appreciation.

Bring home a bunch of inexpensive fresh flowers the next time you go to the grocery store. Separate them and put one or two in each room of your home, including the bathrooms, so that your eye can rest on something beautiful each time you walk into a room.

Wear clothing that makes you feel happy. I have one pair of shoes that my friends all thought I was crazy to buy. They were on sale in an international shoe store and were made in Brazil. The shoes are brown and red platforms with red ties up the front. People never fail to comment on how "unusual" these shoes are, and we inevitably end up laughing. I named them my "happy shoes," and they really are. What pieces of clothing make you feel bright and happy when you put them on? Wear them frequently.

Make sure the movies you go to are uplifting and the messages are beautiful. In this phase of your life, who needs more upset, especially via the very entertainment you seek to relax you? Cut out the murder thrillers, the gruesome films—you get enough of this on the news. Switch the station when the news gets upsetting, or just turn it off. While awareness is important, you don't need constant images of mistreated pets flashing before your eyes every day. This can't help but plummet your mood into darkness. Pull out of it, use beauty as your lifeline, and choose to live beautifully.

Listen to Beautiful Sounds

Music is the obvious auditory vehicle for beauty. Some experts believe that beautiful music, such as the masterpieces of Mozart, can heal both the body and the mind. Described as having a "unique sense of order and clarity," without being overly sentimental, listening to music such as this on a regular basis can help us "reorchestrate" our lives.[4] On the other hand, just as beautiful music can affect your life positively, music that you find unpleasant can make you more anxious and irritable. Change the station on your radio when a song comes on that makes you tense or feels offensive. This is one challenge you don't have to endure.

Our public radio network played a clip called "birdsong" one morning as I was driving to work. A meticulous recording of a different bird vocal was made for each clip. First the birdsong itself was presented, then an explanation of the bird's call, and then a bit about the bird. I know relatively little about birds; I was mesmerized by the beauty of their song and felt totally joyful at hearing this exquisite "music." Italian psychotherapist Piero Ferrucci reports that in his practice, his clients often experience deep healing as a result of hearing the song of birds.[5] Many Italian composers have incorporated birdsong into their compositions, such as Vivaldi's *Cardellino* and Rossini's *La Gazza Ladra.* Why not take a trip to a nearby park, take a seat at a bench for a few moments, and listen to the free music of the birds that surrounds you? Do nothing but appreciate their sound. You should not try to work too hard at appreciating beauty. Just let it happen and enjoy the beauty in each day.

Another way to enjoy beauty in sound is to go to the shore, sit at the edge of the tide, and close your eyes as you drink in the sound of the vibrant waves. The ocean is so symbolic of life. It is mysterious, moody, and beautiful. Listen to all its gifts.

Delight Your Nostrils with Beautiful Smells

On the top of my personal list of beauty are the aromas that came from my Neapolitan grandmother's cooking. I have since re-created her recipes, and I make sure I fill my own kitchen with the comforting familiarity of the cooking aromas that recall those pleasant memories.

Body fragrance is another source of beauty for me. I never liked strong perfumes but do love the subtler natural scents made from essential oils. Lavender is very relaxing for me, as is the renowned gentle scent of Violetta di Parma, a classic fragrance inspired by Maria Luigia, the much-loved Duchess of Parma (1791–1847), whose favorite flower was the violet.

Surround Yourself with Beauty

Pictures, paintings, flowers, pleasantly colored walls, neat working spaces—these are the obvious surroundings where beauty can make a difference. Not so obvious are the *people* you surround yourself with, especially those you invite into your home and into your life. Fill your personal space only with people that add emotional beauty to your existence—those who nurture who you are and honor what you have been through in life. Positive friends are a great source of cheer. Although there are many instances, such as the workplace, where we can't always extricate ourselves from negative people, we can minimize the impact of their ability to affect us. We do this by interacting with them minimally, efficiently, and professionally, and reminding ourselves not to take their upsetting actions or words personally. You have too many exciting things to do right now to be brought down by "ugly" relationships.

Give Your Body a Beauty Makeover

After loss, both men and women can discover greater self-esteem when they have taken action to look their best. Sophia Loren wrote that what really makes a woman beautiful is the belief that she is. She herself insists on four things: quality, lifestyle, color, and self-expression.[6] Tending to these same guidelines can make us feel more beautiful, too.

Picture an average-looking *signorina* (young lady) climbing a hilly cobblestone road one evening in the center of Amalfi. I watched as she struggled and wobbled on her way up, causing onlookers (mostly men) to stand with bated breath and at the ready in case an emergency rescue would be in order. In pursuit of a snack to carry back to my apartment, I ducked into the tiny grocery store, whose display of hot chili peppers was ironically labeled *"viagra naturale."* By the time I emerged with my purchase, the high-heeled *signorina* was negotiating her descent, her skinny, high-heeled boots sinking into gaps between the stones. Now, however, it was an altogether different story: She was perched on the arms of two strong and handsome Italian volunteers. The *signorina* apparently knew something that psychologists have known for some time: dressing attractively gives you confidence. When you feel attractive, you carry yourself in a different way, leading others to find you attractive, too.

To me, a pair of beautiful high heels (or men's shiny dress shoes) signals confidence and victory over loss. When you are at the point where you care about how you look again, you are back in the game. If heels are not your thing, that's okay, too. Just choose items of clothing that make you feel beautiful—a favorite sweater, pretty earrings, textured hosiery. Dig out something you normally save for a special occasion, and wear it to *create* a special occasion. Wear it to the store, to the Laundromat, or to pick up your mail at the post office. Then watch heads turn for you as they did for the *Amalfitana Signorina* with the high-heeled boots. Relish how beautiful you feel!

Gentlemen, you, too, can probably use a bit of spiffing up, as you have probably let your physical appearance slip since your personal crisis. Don't wait. Perk up your wardrobe, comb your hair, shave or trim your beard, get rid of that potbelly if you have one, and send a message to the universe that you are a viable contender for a passionate life. Put some time into pampering yourself, and you will notice the difference in how you feel about yourself. Making only one change can motivate you to carry out an entire series of positive changes.

Good skincare is not gender-specific. I could not live without my bottle of extra-virgin olive oil. In the morning I make a scrub of it with a bit of sugar. I exfoliate my face, elbows, knees, and the backs of my arms with this mixture and rinse it off under a nice hot shower. My skin stays moist and dewy throughout the day. Even my doctor mentioned how great I look when I went in for my checkup. I owe that to this practice. I also use olive oil for the dry ends of my hair, and to massage into my cuticles after I remove my nail polish.

Do-It-Yourself Italian Tips for La Bellezza (Beauty)

Italians love simplicity and freshness, whether it pertains to what they eat or what they put on their skin. Don't forget that your skin is a large porous organ that drinks in what you layer it with. My grandmother always told me not to put anything on my skin that was not good enough to eat. While even I am tempted now and then by Madison Avenue ads for cosmetics and high-priced miracle creams, when I try to read the ingredients on the label, my gut always sends my brain a red flag. Why should I slather my skin with chemicals? (One time, after using a hyped-up moisturizer, I ended up going to a plastic surgeon to remove a small but very visible benign lump on my face.) I always turn back to some Italian basics that have natural benefits, antioxidants, and other nutrients—without the poisons. Here are some of my favorites:

✓ **Basil and olive oil mask.** Externally applied, basil is said to have antiseptic and calming properties. A good extra-virgin olive oil (make sure that it is pure) is a moisturizer second to none, and one that I know will not pollute my skin. This combination is one of my favorites. Start with six organic basil leaves. Rinse, dry on paper towels, then grind; you can use either a mortar and pestle or the back of a wooden spoon and grind the leaves to release the oils. Drizzle enough olive oil (approximately 1 teaspoon) to make a paste and then apply with clean hands to a freshly washed face. Put on your favorite Italian arias as you kick up your heels, close your eyes, and restore your spirit for fifteen minutes, and then rinse with warm water and pat dry. Your skin will feel soft, smooth, and renewed. You can do this up to four times a week.

✓ **Olive-oil body moisturizer.** Olive oil has natural phenols and anti-oxidants. Get rid of all of your synthetic body lotions, no matter how attractive the packaging. Italian beauty comes from the purity of ingredients. This works best after you have just stepped out of the shower or bath and your skin is still warm. Drizzle a bit of extra-virgin olive oil between your palms (I keep a separate bottle in my bathroom for moisturizing purposes), then pat into just-barely towel-dried skin. Pat all over and rub a little extra onto your driest areas, such as elbows, heels, and knees. Contrary to what you might think, this does not leave you greasy; instead you will be silky smooth.

✓ **Tomato hair conditioner.** Tomatoes are filled with lycopene and anti-oxidants. I love how this conditioner makes my hair and scalp feel when I rinse it out. You will need ¼ cup of no-additive tomato puree. After shampooing, rinse hair and then massage the puree into your scalp and hair through to the ends. Leave this in until you wash the rest of your body, shave your legs, etc., then rinse with warm water and finsh with a cool rinse. Your hair will be shiny and bouncy.

✓ **Espresso scrub.** Coffee has recently been found to have some health benefits that were previously unknown. I like to use a coffee scrub on the rough parts of my body, and I often find that a traditional American grind is too rough. Espresso ground coffee is fine enough to slough off the dead cells and leave my skin feeling exuberant. You will need approximately ¼ cup of a good brand of espresso grinds. After washing normally in the shower, sprinkle some of the grinds into your hand or onto the washcloth and gently scrub your knees, the backs of your arms, your heels and ankles, the back of your glutes and thighs, and your elbows. You will be amazed at how energized and beautiful you will feel after you rinse off.

Italian-born hair stylist to the stars Jay Ferrara, whose salon is in Manhattan, deeply believes in making the effort to look good as a way to feel good. According to Jay, who has worked with the most beautiful women in the world, "Body image and physical appearance is [sic] a contributing factor to an individual's self-esteem, and low self-esteem doesn't feel good. Feeling better and more positive about our outward appearances will boost and build confidence, and help us let go of self-doubt."[7]

How do we get that great Italian hair? Ferrara says it doesn't have to cost a lot now to achieve volume and gloss. "Products that were once available to the rich and famous of Hollywood are now quite affordable to the masses," said Jay. "Have fun, experiment, and stick with what works for you."

Make Your Home a Reflection of the Beauty in You

Our home was not a sprawling mansion, but I really loved every inch of the little stone ranch we shared with our children for the last decade of Tom's life. Of course I adorned it with a few meaningful Italian artifacts. A small Italian fresco was carved into the wall over the fireplace. There were built-in book cabinets in which I displayed my favorite books, and we had a huge sunroom into which streamed daylight (or starlight) from all angles, as well as from overhead through the cathedral ceiling pane. Just sitting in that room brought warmth, brightness, and the beauty of a new day. After Tom's death, I moved into a smaller place, and the challenge was to make this new abode feel like a beautiful home sweet home. I made it my mission to place objects of beauty in places where my eyes would rest upon them every time I turned around. Enough change, enough loss. I needed beauty back in my life. Now, when I walk in my front door, I am greeted by a beautiful photo of my maternal grandparents, straight from Italy with their children draped alongside them. One of those children is a dark-eyed, olive-skinned young beauty of about fourteen—my mother, Rachele. Just coming home from work makes me feel like I am being given a hug by the circle of faces that eventually formed mine. As I walk into the dining room there is a modest handwoven basket of Italian straw. In its simplicity—beige with a bright pink-rimmed border on top—it is breathtaking. A surge of happiness streaks through me as I think of how *Zia* Cristina—who is still living in Castelpagano—just recently made that basket for me with her two little hands. Such intricate work, without even having to use eyeglasses! *Zia* is almost ninety.

Beauty looms around every *angolo* (angle) and cobblestone of Italian life. It is no accident that Italians place a high priority on their exposure to beauty. From a careful choice as to what they decide to wear for the day, to the art work and flowers they adorn the insides of their homes with, there is only one reason for the constant Italian thirst for what is beautiful: Beauty makes people feel better. Do all you can to make yours a beautiful life, starting now.

When Ann Marie's husband returned from Afghanistan, she soon realized that the loving man she sent off to war had come back almost a stranger. He now suffered from violent flashbacks and an escalating alcohol problem. She worked hard to be patient and to find resources to help her husband return to the man he once was. Nothing but helping her husband seemed to matter—including her personal upkeep.

Then one day she looked into the mirror and realized she'd let herself go. Her reflection only made her feel defeated.

Josephine didn't know how to get a life of meaning back again after her husband's Alzheimer's progressed to the point that he no longer recognized her. His face took on a look of confusion whenever she visited him in the nursing home. How could it be that the man she had lived with for fifty years now had no clue that he was ever a part of her life? Josephine knew that unless she made some changes in her own life, each day would be a continuum of tears and sadness. She realized she had fallen into an emotional slump. Her posture became hunched, and she looked like she had aged years in a short period of time. People at the nursing home noticed the change in her appearance and commented about how "tired" she looked.

Both Ann Marie and Josephine began to feel better about themselves as soon as they began a good self-care regimen. Pampering and adorning the body with objects of beauty are ancient practices for a reason. These rituals can soften the harshness of your situation by increasing confidence in your ability to get through them. It is not superficial to want to improve your appearance. See yourself as worthy of the effort, because you are.

Taking action to partake in beautiful experiences lifts our hearts and our moods, and these good feelings have positive effects on our health. A large Swedish study of more than 10,000 participants showed that beauty—in the form of attending cultural events—may be associated with longevity. People who regularly went to movies, concerts, and exhibitions had a significantly lower risk of dying as compared to those who did not expose themselves to such beauty.[8]

The gadgets and accessories you choose can also bring beauty into your life. The priority on beauty has even infiltrated the Italian world of the bicycle. According to *Donna* magazine, bicycles are about to become fashion accessories for Italians who want to get around in an eco-friendly, healthy, and economical way.[9] Imagine trying to match your outfit to the signature animal prints of Dolce and Gabbana, the recognizable orange leather trim of Hermes, or making a statement on a Fendi retro all-white sleek two-wheeler. How can you not be prompted to smile?

Feeling good is also beautiful. A simple hot shower followed by a colorful outfit always makes me feel great. Get out of black if you have been in mourning and choose a color that makes you feel happy when you see yourself in it. The other day I bought a chartreuse sweater—bold and totally opposite of anything I had ever worn before, because I was under the impression it would look horrible against my skin. Instead it made me smile and stand up with confidence.

The cycle of loss and gain continues throughout our lives. We had better learn to coexist with this pattern, for as sure as you know your name, on the heels of one, follows the other. We can soften the blows of our losses by caring enough to make ourselves feel and look attractive.

When asked the secret to her physical beauty, Sophia Loren said it is about having an attitude of joy and an inner serenity. Inner peace and outer beauty are a powerful combination to a vibrant new you.

Viva la Tarantella!:
Dance, and Your Heart Will Sing!

*Lo credo infinitamente nel potere del ballo e ritmo come cura, e mi
sono curata da sola anche da una malattia . . . proprio con la danza.*[1]
I infinitely believe in the power of dance to cure, and I even
cured myself from a disease, precisely with dance.

—Alessandra Belloni, Italian singer, percussionist, and tarantella expert

OME PEOPLE DEFINE THEIR LIVES by sorrow for what is gone,
instead of gratitude for the blessings they still have. Loss often
leads to a cautious state of reserve that can easily become confin-
ing. We find it difficult to give ourselves permission to let loose
and begin to laugh and have fun again. We might feel we don't deserve
it, or that we would jinx our own happiness if we begin to express it.
In the Italian culture a balanced life is a sweet life. My Italian relatives
grieve openly when they face loss, but they also move quickly back into

the normal rhythm of their lives. They visit friends, they attend the local *sagra* (seasonal fair), they cook for family, they dance with their grandchildren. It is important to balance our sadness with something that brings us glee. Dancing is one way to create a joyful mood, as joy is its only purpose. I love to have fun and get crazy once in a while, with the healing power of an Italian tarantella.

Imagine how you would feel if you just jumped up right now and went into a tarantella, trancelike dance. Most likely, even visualizing this is enough to perk you up. A lively, heart-thumping Italian tarantella, which some say may date back to the Middle Ages or even earlier (perhaps to 2000 BC) can't help but jolt your mood back to happy as your body gets lively and your momentum gets going.

Dance as a Source of Healing

The tarantella is, by design, a frenzied folk dance done to a quick upbeat tempo and accompanied by tambourine. The combination of jingles combined with upbeat music, twirling, and quickness of step can rejuvenate a sullen mood. Centuries ago, healers would prescribe the tarantella as a remedy for tarantism, the hysterical state supposedly induced by the poisonous bite of the tarantula spider. It was said that fast-paced dancing would help a person sweat the toxins out. The tarantella was actually believed to restore both physical and mental health. Today, there is considerable research suggesting that the sheer joy of dance can even treat depression.[2]

When I was in my freshman year of college, and before Tom and I were exclusively dating each other, I was walking to my Wednesday cello class when I heard some music by Emerson, Lake, and Palmer coming from one of the piano practice rooms. I peeked in, and there was a small crowd of female fans around the pianist, *ooh*-ing and *ah*-ing. "Robert" was Native American, artsy-looking, and handsome: long black hair parted down the middle and an even-toothed smile that never tired. The other thing—besides his musical talent—that attracted me to him was the way he made each of his listeners feel important. I became one of them. When he caught me looking in at him through the little window of the door, he motioned with his head for me to enter. Before long I was sitting on the bench next to him and playing a duet. I could have sworn by the way he looked back at me that he was smitten, too.

"Want to play some more on Saturday?" he asked as we prepared to leave that day.

Who wouldn't? "Sure," I replied. We agreed to meet at 10:30 AM at the piano in the basement of the student center.

To be honest, I could barely think of anything else between that Wednesday and Saturday. All I did was imagine playing the piano with Robert, making beautiful music together, talking about deep things, like the meaning of life (hey, it was the '70s) and sitting right alongside him on the piano bench jamming. My young heart really did seem to grow wings, as cliché as that might sound. That is, until he stood me up.

When Saturday finally came I stood for almost two hours at the piano where we were to meet. Then I went to the piano rooms in the music building just in case one of us had miscommunicated. Finally I called his house. He was obviously not alone and acted like he didn't even know who I was.

Later that day, my mother saw me sulking in the living room. Without saying a word, she went over to the turntable, and before long, some upbeat Italian music was blasting from our stereo. I told her to stop as it was annoying me and disturbed my sullen thoughts. But instead, she grabbed me by the wrist and pulled me out of my chair and onto my feet and began dancing wildly around me, coaxing me to join in. She put one foot in front of the other, arm looped into mine, twirling about in a whirling dervish-inducing euphoria. I started to laugh, as this whole thing was nuts. Then I began twirling Mamma around until *she* had finally had enough. We practically collapsed in giggles, and I had hardly thought about Robert again. That burst of lively dancing really balanced me and pulled me out of my self-pity. While there are many reasons I am grateful to my Italian family, the ability to turn a sad heart into a glad one is a skill for which I will always be indebted to them.

Admittedly, not everyone happens to have tarantella music at hand, but if you can spare ninety-nine cents for the Amazon download, I highly recommend it! For a more classic twist, check out Rossini, who is among the great composers who incorporated the tarantella in their music.

Tarantella music never fails to perk me up when I need it. Any lively music, though, can have the same effect. If you are willing to go for it, play an instrument at the same time you are dancing. Percussion instruments are typically used during tarantella dances. I don't own a tambourine, but an old shoe box works just fine as a makeshift drum.

Just the motion of whirling about gets rid of negative energy. The whirling dervishes, originally a Sufi order made up of followers of the thirteenth century Persian poet Rumi, twirled as a form of prayer. As early as the twelfth century, Tibetans used twirling as part of their yoga practice to keep a fit mind and body. I prefer dancing to twirling, as straight twirling makes me dizzy. The Italian tarantella involves hopping, skipping, and the right amount of twirling, percussion, and music all wrapped into one. Dancing (either by yourself or with your friends) is a tool you can use to pull yourself out of an emotional slump. The important thing is that you dance on a regular basis. If the tarantella is too fast-paced, even ballroom dance has been shown to have a positive effect on mood.[3] I now reserve at least one evening a week as my time for dancing.

Some research confirms that *group* dance also has a powerful positive effect on depression. Depression is called the common cold of mental illness by those in the mental health field. It affects 121 million people worldwide, according to the World Health Organization, and the costs go beyond a personal loss of joy.[4] A study conducted at the University of Heidelberg compared three groups with respect to the effects of group dance on clinical depression. One group of patients was assigned to a dance group performing a traditional upbeat circle dance. A second group just listened to the dance music. A third group was assigned to move on an exercise bicycle to the same level of arousal as the dance group. While in all three groups depression was stabilized, there was significantly less depression in the dance group compared to the other two. The study concluded that stimulating circle dances have a positive effect on depression.[5]

Roman-born Alessandra Belloni is a singer, dancer, percussionist, and renowned expert of the Southern Italian tarantella. She deeply believes in the power of the tarantella to heal both body and mind. Belloni's passion is teaching Southern Italian ritual dances, which have been used as music and dance therapy for centuries throughout the Mediterranean. Participants learn the unique style of tambourine playing and the ancient healing trance dance of the tarantella as part of the program. Belloni's students find they can reduce stress and reconnect to their spiritual energy because of the *maestra's* (master's) teachings.

Belloni isn't the only one who believes in the healing properties of dance. In a recent article published in *AARP*, dance was mentioned as a healing tool for everything from cardiovascular health to dementia.[6] The combination of intellectual and social stimulation was credited for the healing power of dance. Dance was first recognized as having therapeutic value in the 1940s, when Marian Chace used dance to help traumatized war veterans in St. Elizabeth's Hospital in Washington, DC, a federal psychiatric hospital where she taught "Dance for Communication." An accomplished dancer herself, she began to notice that many students who came to her to learn to dance were not in it to become performers. She became the first full-time "dance therapist" when doctors, hearing what a special teacher she was, began sending patients to her.[7] While dance therapy is used in professional contexts to heal a number of physical and emotional challenges, the benefits of dance are available to everyone, and you don't have to be in a therapeutic setting to avail yourself of them.

The effectiveness of self-help strategies is not to be minimized. Just going out to dance on your own, or even in your living room, yields immediate, noticeable results for most people. The integration of movement, music, and felicity combine into a powerful experience of personal renewal.

The tarantella, of course, is not the only kind of dance that can reconnect you to joy. In a pilot study of depression in older adults in the community, researchers from the University of Nevada used ballroom dance lessons as the intervention. The intervention group received instruction in the fox-trot, waltz, swing, and other traditional forms of ballroom dance. The results of this study found that ballroom dance lessons increased a sense of self-efficacy (self-confidence) and lifted hopelessness—two factors that are very much related to depression. Best of all, the subjective experience of formerly depressed participants was positive and one of enjoying the experience of dance.[8]

Several months after I lost Tom, I saw an announcement for a group ballroom dance event a few towns from where I lived. Just two lines embedded in the classified section, and I can't even tell you what made me circle the ad. I did circle it, though, and then put the paper down. The ad gave a phone number and the address of a local Italian civic club. I thought about it for the entire week before finally deciding to go, not knowing what to expect. I had never done something like that before, and it would be my first time out socially since my whole world had been turned upside down. I had more than a bit of trepidation, but I knew how dance used to cheer me up from the time I was a little girl enrolled in dance lessons.

The evening of the dance arrived, and I stood at the entrance of a spacious ballroom hall warmed by the dim glow of chandeliers and a silver ball reflecting specks of light that moved across the walls and floor. I paused for a few minutes, to watch the dancers floating gracefully around the perimeter of the room, to the smooth vocals of Frank Sinatra. The dancers were welcoming and friendly. This debut into the world of ballroom dance was my first major turning point toward the direction of a new life. I had truly let go of the heaviest of my grief. Despite my trepidation, I walked onto the dance floor that evening and began to blend in. I did not remember any particular ballroom steps, but that hardly mattered. I felt like I had been lifted up to the heavens on a cloud.

While dancing by yourself is not to be discounted as a way to lift your mood, the social interaction of group dancing can also provide an emotionally safe environment, the opportunity to make new acquaintances, and a chance to listen to music that makes you feel carefree. Whether traditional folk dance, ballroom, tap, disco, or ballet, dance is one ingredient in the Italian recipe for *allegria* (jubilance).

Here are some ways you can let the sweetness of Italian dance inebriate you with delight:

✓ Purchase some inexpensive Italian tarantella music and dance consistently. There is a ninety-nine-cent tarantella medley sold on Amazon, recorded by the Roman Holiday Ensemble. You can download it as an MP3 file, and let it perk you up when you play it. Play it often, and dance along with it, at least once a day. Dance whenever you are in a slump or when another wave of grief takes you off balance.

✓ Learn a few tarantella (or any other dance) steps. There are three ways to learn dance besides taking lessons.

   ✓ Verbal instructions: ehow.com (type: tarantella dance steps).

   ✓ Visual instruction: www.youtube.com (type: tarantella Napoletana or tarantella Siciliana, and so on). There are different regional styles of this joyful dance.

   ✓ Workshop instruction: www.alessandrabelloni.com. Dr. Belloni offers wonderful tarantella workshops in, where else—the *bel paese,* beautiful Italy.

✓ Take a group ballroom dance lesson. Just give it a try. Type "local ballroom dance events" for your area into Google or Yahoo search engines. You can also find dance classes on Meetup.com. These are inexpensive and unintimidating classes where you can get the wonderful feeling of dressing up to dance and interacting with lovely people who share a common bond.

Dance moves revitalize you, revive your energy, and confirm that not every task has to have a goal to be important. Happiness is one of the most important objectives of all. There are no excuses not to let the joy of dance become a part of your personal renaissance.

La Creatività: Use Your Creativity to Create a New Life

Dobbiamo cambiare mentalità.
We must change our mentality.

—Valerio Albisetti, psychoanalyst, professor, author

THE REAL GENIUS OF LEONARDO DA VINCI, according to author Michael Gelb, was not just in what he created, but in what he can inspire us to create.[1] Everyday creativity is not just for geniuses, nor is it a recent phenomenon. Creativity is simply the desire to concretize and share the ideas from deep within you. It is a profound expression of your inner potential. Since the dawn of time, humans have left evidence of their creativity, confirming our instinctual passion for translating unique ideas into concrete artifacts that are then put out there in the world. What remains of our ancestors' creativity reflects the entire spectrum of emotions, from inner playfulness to spirituality, agony, celebration, sorrow, and anger. Theirs was an attempt to communicate what they believed in, who they were, and what they stood for. The universal nature of creativity gives us a sense of continuity across time, and a sense we are not alone. Italian author and psychotherapist Piero Ferrucci wrote: "There is no better therapy than creative expression."[2] I witnessed this firsthand when the day came for my grandfather and me to head back to the States from our visit to Italy.

My cousin l'artista Michele De Filippo (Girifalco 1913–1990) wiped his eyes as *nano* (Grandfather) and I prepared to leave Calabria. Michele had waited so long to be reunited with his *zio* (uncle) (my grandfather) and me that to part with us again caused him uncontrollable sorrow. He cried unabashedly and begged us to stay, to live there permanently. The best we could do was promise that we would be back again. The obvious yet unspoken reality was that considering my grandfather's advanced age, this would probably be his last visit.

"Wait. Before you leave," he said as he took my hand, "I want you to sit for a portrait." I rarely like to have my picture taken, let alone have my portrait painted. Michele insisted, however, so I obeyed. He positioned me on the side of an old wooden chair that was way past its prime. My right arm was draped over the chair, and Michele gently turned my face to one side and asked me to turn just my eyes toward him. Afraid to move so as to not prolong the process, I watched the artist tear a sheet of brown paper (not unlike that of a paper grocery bag), from a roll and clip it to his easel. He squeezed some paints onto his palette, mixed a few blobs of color together like a cook who needed no recipe but used instinct to create a culinary masterpiece, then he turned his head to study me. I was at an age when I was still deeply self-conscious about my flaws, and I prayed he would just get on with it and turn back to his easel. He didn't.

Not for a long while. In fact, he rose from his chair and walked over to me, as if in a stupor, eyes affixed as he ever-so-precisely repositioned me. Moving me with barely detectable nuances in the angle and pose, he kept at it until I was in the exact position where the sunlight from the little window, in an otherwise dark studio, would set only my face aglow. That day, I came to realize that just being in the presence of creativity was a sacred experience. Michele was sharing his heart, soul, mind, talent—all of him, in order to communicate his love. In those moments, God himself seemed to be guiding Michele's hand with exquisite perfection.

In those hours, I took note as Michele walked back and forth from his easel to where I sat in stillness. He prepared his brushes over and over with much *pazienza* (patience), took another careful look at me, and put more pigment to paper. I don't know how much time elapsed; in reality Michele was a very accomplished artist, and it probably didn't take long at all. Even if it had taken all day and then some, I wouldn't have noticed. I had become so engrossed in the process of how this artist transformed the sadness of saying good-bye to us into a tangible object of joy that would remain in my life forever.

Through his example, Michele showed me how important it is to get in touch with our gifts, develop them, and turn them into creative expressions of love. The painting had to dry, of course, and I wasn't allowed to see it until I went home. He handed it to me all scrolled up with a rubber band to keep it from unraveling in my suitcase. Many years later, this portrait still hangs by my desk, and its meaning for me goes to the very nexus of who I am. I will always be a part of that little town of Girifalco, and of that day when I was together with my grandfather and Michele. Although those moments can never be reproduced (both great men have since passed on), the essence of Michele's creativity made that day eternal. It made me realize that our creativity is what leads us to who we really are and all that we are meant to be in this life. During the Renaissance, the fresco was the preferred painting technique. According to historian Paul Johnson in his book *The Renaissance: A Short History*, the process required enormous patience. Artists had to think of every detail of their projects in advance because of the materials that were used. They had to draw countless *disegni* (designs) in advance of the final work, because once the final work was in progress, an artist could not go back and correct any emergent mistakes. In working on the fresco itself, there were a number of potential frustrations. For instance, mixing pigments with egg yolk, as was done in that time, had its drawbacks: Some pigments had to be excluded all together. The paint had to be applied thinly or the work could be ruined. It was difficult to paint so smoothly that the brushstrokes would be invisible. Creating shadows created even more problems. Every work took a long time, from initial thought through the preparatory stage to palette choices to final masterpiece.[3] Yet those artists persevered in the spirit of creative expression, a force greater than themselves. Creativity gives the world a glimpse into one's soul.

Let Creativity Lead You to Your Personal Renaissance

Many historic Italian figures are still familiar to us today for having left the mark of their creativity on the world. Centuries later we still recognize the names of Da Vinci, Michelangelo, Dante, Aurelio, Vivaldi, Toscanini, Giotto, and many others. In developing their passion, talent, and skill, they were able to leave a lasting impression that still moves us to pleasure today.

Creativity is a way to express your talents, dreams, and desires. It unites your thoughts, feelings, and actions to represent who you really are. Use it to clarify this new wonderful phase in your life in which you have unlimited potential. What you produce with your unique talents and ideas can make a real contribution to some segment of the world around you. You don't have to create a masterpiece and you don't have to be a genius to allow creativity to give your life a meaning that goes far beyond your heartaches and losses.

Here are some ways to revel in your own creative abilities:

✓ Think of things you love to make. Examples might be sweetbreads, textiles, jewelry, desserts, music, poetry, flower arrangements, sweaters, portraits, sculptures, speeches.

✓ Consider reconnecting to some creative activities you did in the past but have lost touch with over the years. Examples could be: writing short stories, playing the piano, writing songs, or acting in local plays.

✓ Pursue creative experiences you have always wanted to try. Examples might be: writing a mystery novel, making a video documentary, publishing an Op-Ed piece, starting a small business, or getting a product idea patented and sold.

Each day, engage in one item from the first category, and begin to work on one item from the other two categories. Get the training or preparation you need so you will have the tools to create what your unique mind can conceive of. There are people who need to benefit from the inspiration of your creativity.

Live a Creative Life

My mother, Rachele, had many creative talents, one of which was making pies. Rachele loved to bake and try out different dessert recipes. When someone in the neighborhood was ill, in mourning, had family problems, or was going through any kind of personal crisis, she would bring a pie to console them. My mother also tapped into her creativity through sewing, knitting, and playing Italian songs on the piano. She did these activities almost effortlessly and they brought her great happiness. One sunny afternoon I was by her side as she dedicated herself to the careful creation of an Italian cream pie that we would later bring to my aunt, who had just gotten out of the hospital. My mother hadn't been feeling well herself that day and probably could have used a rest. Instead, she said, she always felt better when she was able to make something for someone else. My mother's most important qualities were her cheerfulness and generosity toward others.

When the pie was done that day, we went for a visit. I remember the delight on my aunt's face as we walked through the door with the mouthwatering dessert in hand. Mamma shuffled around in my aunt's kitchen for a while until she found the *macchinetta* (the Italian espresso maker) and the foil espresso coffee bag. The clinking of dishes, cups, and silverware promptly lent sound to our festivity as we set my aunt's table and filled her kitchen with the magnificent aroma of the rich coffee beans. My aunt beamed from ear to ear as my mother went to the piano and chimed out songs that all three of us could sing along to. In less than an hour, Mamma created a carefree afternoon in which all troubles just faded away.

You don't have to be Bernini or Brunelleschi to create something extraordinary. You can even create that Italian cream pie that Mamma made that day. Before she died, I begged her to write down the recipe for me. The little index card, now yellowed with age, is covered with her handwriting and is one of my most treasured artifacts, as is the memory of that afternoon when her creation of a simple pie brought laughter and healing. Your assignment—should you accept it—is to make a happy occasion of baking this pie. Put on some music, put your whole heart and soul into it, and then share it with someone who can use some cheering up. Think of what an unexpected joy you will give someone you care about! Perhaps it will be someone who has just received some bad news. Your creativity can make a difference for them, as it will for you.

Rachele's Italian Cream Pie

MAKES 8–10 SERVINGS

Filling:

6 egg yolks

1 cup sugar

1 quart plus 1 cup milk

5 tablespoons cornstarch

¾ cup flour

1 teaspoon vanilla

1 teaspoon lemon extract

1 lemon rind, grated (just the yellow)

Crust:

2 cups all-purpose flour

¼ teaspoon salt

1 teaspoon baking powder

½ cup sugar

3 egg yolks

1 teaspoon vanilla

3 tablespoons shortening

1. **To make the filling:** Beat the egg yolks until creamy. Add the sugar, milk, cornstarch, flour, vanilla, lemon extract, and lemon rind. In a medium saucepan, cook the mixture over medium heat, stirring carefully until it thickens like pudding. Lower the heat as needed so as not to let the cream burn. When thickened, remove from the heat and cool.

2. **To make the crust:** Mix the flour, salt, baking powder, and sugar together (dry ingredients). Add the egg yolks and vanilla, then cut in the shortening. When the dough forms, divide into two balls, one just slightly larger for the bottom crust, which you will roll out on a floured dough board or a clean section of your counter or table that has been dusted with flour. Roll the slightly larger ball into a 12-inch inch circle. Place into a greased 10-inch glass pie plate, then pour the cooled filling in. Roll out the smaller ball of dough into a 10-inch circle, then cut into strips. Crisscross the strips over the top of the pie. Bake in a preheated 325°F oven for 45 minutes or until the top is golden.

Creative Healing

When Charlie came home from the Middle East, one leg didn't make it back with him. He had no idea how he would fit back into society because of his disability. Eventually he was able to walk with a prosthetic leg. Nothing was the same, but he turned his hardship into inner growth. He saw people and things differently, and his priorities became very clear. The fragility of his life and the lives of others was something he had not given too much thought to before he was sent off to war. Now he has a new sense of gratitude for what he still has in his life and for the people he loves.

In Charlie's darkest hour, he found solace in creating hummingbird feeders. He had always loved to watch hummingbirds as a boy. With his natural knack for understanding the way things work, Charlie figured out how to recycle plastic drinking bottles and bottle caps of different sizes and create a makeshift hummingbird feeder. He found directions for a nectar concoction on the Internet, which he used to fill the feeder. He hung his first creation right outside his home office window where he could observe and delight in the little buzzing creatures. He watched as their wings flapped so fast they seemed to suspend themselves in midair. As they came back and forth to fill up on nectar, Charlie created more feeders with recycled plastic bottles. He gave one to everyone who visited him after his injury. The visitors, who came bearing gifts for Charlie, were instead surprised and delighted to receive these special handmade gifts. Several people called weeks later to say how much enjoyment they got whenever they sat outside from watching the birds feeding from these little devices. The flight of the hummingbirds became their main summer entertainment, and whenever they watched the spectacle, they thought of Charlie's loving kindness.

I, too, used creativity to heal. When I was ready, I knew I had to create something good from the trauma of my loss. I decided I would use my talents as a speaker, self-help specialist, and writer for supporting people through their toughest challenges. As my first holiday season without Tom drew near, I went on television and gave tips, based on what worked for me, on how to get through the holidays after a devastating loss. Just months later, I gave a presentation at a major hotel chain on rebuilding a life after loss. People began to gravitate toward me. They wanted more; they found comfort in my words, and I continued to evolve even further in helping others to feel better about their challenges. Soon I brought back my radio show "The Art of Living Well," which is made up of tips, ideas, and interviews that inspire listeners and give them hope. I started a self-help blog, where I give hundreds of free tips for making life sweeter, as was my intention with my original book, *Living la Dolce Vita: Bring the Passion, Laughter, and Serenity of Italy into Your Daily Life.*[4] I was motivated to write the book you are reading now, because I knew that I had the ability to touch people's lives. This book is my creative gift to you.

Create Your Personal Renaissance

To create your own personal renaissance, start with the same process the fresco artists used: Begin with contemplative forethought followed by the preparation of sketching out a vision of how you want your life to be within the context of your reality today. Select your "palette" of steps and the activities that will lead you there, then take action until you have fully reclaimed your life after loss.

The term *renaissance* describes a period of transition between medieval times and the modern age. It was a cultural rebirth that marked the beginning of a new, hopeful era. Now you have taken yourself fully out of the darkness of your trauma. Think of yourself as proof that a bright new renaissance is possible. Because of what you have been through, you have gained a deeper understanding of what it means to be alive, and a deeper appreciation of that which before you may have taken for granted. Let your present existence reflect your true potential. Live with joy and unabashed passion. Discover your inner strengths and your capacity to transform your life into an amazing journey of new adventures, new talents, new hobbies, new you.

In the privacy of your living room make time to turn on the music and create a new dance. Cook a delicious Italian meal for friends, ad-libbing the ingredients. Perhaps you have carpentry skills and can build a table out of a tree trunk. Get back to a hobby you have let go for years such as crocheting doilies, cutwork embroidery, or fixing up vintage cars. If you are a great conversationalist then get out and get a dialogue going with someone who gets no visitors in a nursing home. Try your hand at writing a simple love poem for someone special. Create a CD for a friend who loves the same music as you. Let your imagination flow, and watch how you discover endless routes to happiness.

Make a list of the people in your life who have been there for you, especially throughout the crisis you have recently faced. Show them your appreciation with a special gift that you create just for them. It may take months to get through your list, but loyal relationships are worth their weight in gold.

Your Personal Renaissance Template

Fill in your own ideas to become the architect of the new life you desire. What will your personal renaissance look like? You can follow this road map to getting there.

✓ Contemplate and plan your *disegno* (design). Take as long as you need to on this phase. Doing the work up front, as the fresco artists had to do, will save you a lot of backtracking later. Consider the areas of life that are most important to you. You can modify the bullet points below to include or exclude anything you want.

✓ If you could snap your fingers and create masterpieces in the following areas, describe what those masterpieces would look like:

➡ Health	➡ Family	➡ Spirituality
➡ Work/Career	➡ Friends	➡ Venue (where you
➡ Relationships	➡ Creative	want to live this
➡ Love partner	expressions	part of your life)

✓ Choose your palette (the step you will take to reach your dream life). Below are some examples:

➡ Health—make appointments for your regular checkups; pick out a fitness plan and schedule it into your day, start a meditation program to reduce your stress.

➡ Work/Career—Take a free course on starting your own business; look for a new job that better reflects who you are now; network with other professionals; join the local chamber of commerce to meet new people and advance your career.

➡ Relationships:

— Love partner—Join a reputable online dating site; join a local singles group; improve your current relationship; decide to stay single and explore that for a while.

— Family—Let family members know how much you love them; draw boundaries by asking family members for what you need from them; contact extended family for regular get-togethers; conduct an ancestry search and reunite with relatives you have never met.

— Friends—Let go of negative friendships; strengthen good friendships through more regular contact and thoughtful gestures; make new friends by asking good acquaintances to get together for a cup of coffee.

→ Creative expressions—Engage in creative activities, either those you previously enjoyed or new ones.

→ Spirituality—Explore the benefits of strengthening your belief in a higher power; read sacred texts, immerse yourself in sacred venues (churches, synagogues, or others).

→ Venue—Gather information about a country or state you always wanted to live in; make your current living quarters neat, clean, and beautiful if you choose to stay where you are.

Abraham Maslow, the great humanist psychologist, identified creativity as among the highest of human needs. Creativity requires patience and authenticity. The idea is not just to have fantastical ideas swimming around in your head, but to figure out how to translate them into concrete manifestations that will bring you satisfaction and others great happiness. Creativity is a pathway to achieving your greatest potential.

Epilogo: Turn Your Life's Lemons into Limoncello

Books that distribute things . . . with as daring a freedom
as we use in dreams, put us on our feet again.
—Marsilio Ficino, Humanist philosopher and astrologer (1433–1499)

I DON'T KNOW WHERE I WOULD BE in times of personal crises had it
not been for the insights I gleaned from my Italian cultural heritage. Through the example and words of those who came before
me, I was able to avoid total despair and transform my life into an
even greater gift. In my darkest hours, when I thought I could not take
another step, I would think of my grandparents, and be reminded of the
courageous way they approached life through word and deed. The visits
back and forth to Italy over the years, first with my grandfather and then
alone to visit family members, gave me insights into the real meaning of
resilience and the importance of participating in the ordinary, soothing
rituals that bring the human spirit to exultation: a midafternoon visit

to a friend's home to say *buon giorno* (hello); a *sfogliatelle* (Neapolitan pastry) at the café where you are a regular; a little patch of garden where the sweat you poured into it has sprouted fragrant blooms of color to delight you.

Journalist Luigi Barzini noted (in his brilliant book *The Italians*) some characteristics of the Italian people, which observers often remark about: a determination that is stronger than hardship, a cheerfulness toward others, a lack of boredom or malaise, a passion for celebrating life. Yet these are also people who have gone through personal and collective tragedy. Over the years, my time in Italy has reunited me with family and friends who live ordinary lives with extraordinary tranquility. They face the same personal and political crises we all do, but their everyday resilience is fueled by the uncomplicated pleasures that confirm what a gift it is to be alive.

I also draw resilience from Italian geniuses of the past. The ability of exquisite music, art, literature, and philosophy to lift my heart in times of challenges and shine a light on the pathway out of pain is not to be underestimated. The Roman philosophers gave me just the right words to pull myself out of self-destructive moods. Renaissance artists lifted my spirits and motivated me to develop my talents, too. Even the mysterious Etruscans left behind artifacts most likely used for festivities, illustrating the importance of living life to the fullest.

As a young professor, I once taught a psychology class on lifespan development. To make the material more real, I asked my students to draw a hypothetical time line of their own lives, starting with their birthdates and ending with the projected date they hoped to live to. I asked them to mark the dates of the most important events of their lives up to this point. Many students added happy, meaningful times. A first holy communion, a Sweet Sixteen birthday party. Others included tragic events, such as the death of one of their parents or a diagnosis of their own life-threatening illness.

Everyone's time line was similar, albeit the particulars were very different. We have all enjoyed momentous occasions and hopefully we will be blessed for many more. Likewise, we have all suffered seemingly impossible challenges—yet we made it through those, too. My real question, however, was, "How are you filling your life in between those noteworthy markers?" Whatever it is, make every precious minute count!

The essence of Italian life is to make oneself happy with what is, and not insist that life be anything other than that. Italian resilience comes from a full acceptance of what it means to love, lose, and live once again.

Consider the advice of Roman stoic philosopher Seneca: "Set aside a certain number of days during which you shall be content with the scantiest and cheapest fare, with coarse and rough dress, saying to yourself the while: 'Is this the condition that I feared?'"[1]

The trauma of your loss is now behind you. You already know what it means to be without someone or some aspect of your life that you never thought you could. You made it. You have nothing else to fear.

Let the traditional Italian values of love, balance, and simplicity help you experience a personal renaissance. Put joy and hope into *this* day, *this* moment. Italy is a culture that relishes modest daily indulgences that are often shared in company. You will always land back on your feet if you live this way.

Let us open up our hearts again and resculpt, repaint, or rewrite our life's story. Yes, we have a past, and hopefully we will have a future, but the present is the only clay available for shaping now. Day by day you can create a life that is an inspiration to others and a font of joy for yourself. Let each day be a testimony to love, family, good food and wine, arts, music, God, and the unassuming wonders of all you have been blessed with.

Let us raise a glass to your bright new beginning.

Tante belle cose,

Raeleen

Notes

Introduction

1. Long, G., trans. 2006. *The Meditations of Marcus Aurelius*. London: Sacred Wisdom, p. 119.

Chapter 1

1. Albisetti, V. 2005. *Come Attraversare la Sofferenza: E Uscirne Più Forti*. Milano: Paoline, p. 22.

2. Bonaguidi, F., C. Michelassi, F. Filipponi, and D. Rovai. 2010. Religiosity Associated with Prolonged Survival in Liver Transplant Recipients. *Liver Transplantation* 16(10):1158–63.

3. Meli, E. 2010. Credere in Dio Allunga la Vita. *Il Corriere della Sera*. http://www.corriere .it/salute/10_ottobre_16/fede-dio-allunga-vita-religione-meli_31e3a57c-d5e9-11df-a0eb -00144f02aabc.shtml.

4. http://www.umbertoeco.com/en/.

5. Special Eurobarometer 225 Report. 2005. *Social Values, Science & Technology*, February, p. 9.

6. Griffiths, P. J. 1999. *Religious Reading: The Place of Reading in the Practice of Religion*. New York: Oxford University Press. In Preface.

7. Pennebaker, J. W. 1993. Putting Stress into Words: Health, Linguistic, and Therapeutic Implications. *Behavior Research and Therapy* 31:539–548.

8. ANSA. 2012. Meditare fa bene alla salute, meno stress meno infiammazioni: La psicoterapia punta sui neurotrasmettitori delle emozioni. May 25. http://www.ansa .it/saluteebenessere/notizie/rubriche/stilidivita/2012/05/25/Meditare-fa-bene-salute-meno -stress-meno-infiammazioni_6931344.html.

9. CBS News Video. 2010. *Brain Boosting Changes Body.* http://www.cbsnews.com/video/watch/
?id=6295572n&tag=contentMain;contentBody.

Chapter 2

1. Helmore, E. 2011. Interview, Andrea Bocelli: The World Famous Tenor on His Faith, His
Critics and Why Blindness Is No Obstacle. http://www.radiotimes.com/news/2011-10-02/
interview-andrea-bocelli.

2. Willingham, V. 2009. The Power of Music: It's a Real Heart Opener. http://www.cnn.com/2009/
HEALTH/05/11/music.heart/index.html.

3. Yun, S. H., and W. Gallant. 2010. Evidence-Based Clinical Practice: The Effectiveness of Music-
Based Intervention for Women Experiencing Forgiveness/Grief Issues. *Journal of Evidence
Based Social Work* 7(5):361–76.

4. Siedliecki, S. L., and M. Good. 2006. Effect of Music on Power, Pain, Depression and Disability.
Journal of Advanced Nursing 54(5):553–62.

5. Kreutz G., S. Bongard, S. Rohrmann, V. Hodapp, and D. Grebe. 2004. Effects of Choir Singing or Listening on Secretory Immunoglobulin A, Cortisol, and Emotional State. *Journal of
Behavioral Medicine* 27(6):623–635.

6. http://www.pensieriparole.it/frasi/leopold-fechtner/.

Chapter 3

1. http://www.manuscritto.it/aforismi_uomo.html.

2. http://www.youtube.com/watch?v=uqLSCRCw8l0.

3. Hyman, M. 2012. Why Doing Nothing Is the Key to Happiness. *Huffington Post.* http://www
.huffingtonpost.com/dr-mark-hyman/meditation-tips_b_1620411.html.

4. Mondelli, M. 2008. Quality of Life: The Italian Siesta. *Huffington Post.* http://www.huffington
post.com/marta-mondelli/quality-of-life-the-itali_b_152715.html.

Chapter 4

1. Ellis, A., and R. Harper. 1975. *A New Guide To Rational Living* (3rd ed). Chatsworth, CA:
Willshire Book Co.

2. Maslow, A. H. 1994. *Religions, Values, and Peak Experiences.* New York: Penguin Books.

3. McLean, K. 2012. The Healing Art of Meditation. http://www.yalescientific.org/2012/05/the
-healing-art-of-meditation/.

4. Chan, A. 2011. Why Mindfulness Makes Us Healthier. *The Huffington Post.* http://www.huffingtonpost.com/2011/11/02/mindfulness-meditation-health_n_1070101.html.

Chapter 5

1. Bonanno, G. A. 2004. Loss, Trauma, and Human Resilience: Have We Underestimated the Human Capacity to Thrive After Extremely Aversive Events? *American Psychologist* 59:20–28.

2. Ibid.

3. Ibid.

4. Seligman, M. E. P. 1975. *Helplessness: On Depression, Development, and Death.* San Francisco: W. H. Freeman.

Chapter 6

1. Plumb, J. H. 2001. *The Italian Renaissance.* New York: Houghton Mifflin.

2. Ibid., p. 236.

3. Keen, S. 1974. The Golden Mean of Roberto Assagioli. *Psychology Today,* Dec., p. 97–107.

4. Assagioli, R. 2008. *Transpersonal Development.* English Translation. UK: Smiling Wisdom.

Chapter 7

1. The Institute of Psychosynthesis. 2012. Psychosynthesis psychology. http://www.psychosynthesis.org/html/articles.htm.

2. Ferrucci, P. 2009. *Beauty and the Soul: The Extraordinary Power of Everyday Beauty to Heal Your Life.* New York: Penguin.

3. Ibid.

4. Ibid.

5. De Tommaso, M., M. Sardaro, and P. Livrea. 2008. Aesthetic Value of Paintings Affects Pain Thresholds. *Consciousness and Cognition* 17:1152–1162.

6. Ferrucci, P. (2009). *Beauty and the Soul: The extraordinary power of everyday beauty to heal your life.* New York: Penguin.

7. Plumb, J. H. 2001. *The Italian Renaissance.* New York: Houghton Mifflin.

8. Carroll, N. 2003. Art and the Mind. *The Monist* 86(4):521–555.

9. Tranquilli, A. L., A. Luccarini, and M. Emanuelli. 2007. The Creation of Adam and God-placenta. *Journal of Maternal-Fetal, and Neotatal Medicine* 20(2):83–87.

10. Veninga, R. 2011. Vital Speeches of the Day. Nov 1, 2011. Caring for Ourselves as We Care for Others: The Psychology of Resilience.

11. Ibid.

12. *Automobile Magazine.* 2009. Five Minutes with Fabrizio. http://www.automobilemag.com/features/0308_fabrizio/.

Chapter 8

1. Aurelius, M. 2006. *The Meditations of Marcus Aurelius.* Translated by George Long. London: Sacred Wisdom, p. 41.

2. Seligman, M. E. P. 2006. *Learned Optimism: How to Change Your Mind and Change Your Life.* New York: Vintage Books.

3. Brewer, J. A., J. H. Davis, and J. Goldstein. 2012. *Why Is It So Hard to Pay Attention, or Is It? Mindfulness: The Factors of Awakening and Reward-Based Learning.* New York: Springer Science and Business Media.

4. Nadolny, M. 2012. Angelini Raises a Glass to Simplicity. *The Day,* CT. http://www.theday.com/article/20120318/ENT04/303189989/1044.

5. Provoledo, E. 2012. I'm Staying in Rome Is the New Theme for Summer Vacation. http://www.nytimes.com/2012/08/15/world/europe/italys-beaches-short-on-la-dolce-vita.html?pagewanted=all&_r=0.

6. *Corriere della Sera.* 2012. Il Flusso di Mail al Lavoro? Uno stress. http://www.corriere.it/salute/cardiologia/12_maggio_07/email-stress_c3e874c8-984f-11e1-b99c-a30fdbaea52f.shtml.

Chapter 9

1. Aurelius, M. 2006. *The Meditations of Marcus Aurelius.* Translated by George Long. London: Sacred Wisdom.

2. Ibid., p. 112.

3. Bonanno, G. A. 2005. Resilience in the face of potential trauma. *Current Directions in Psychological Science* 14(3):135–138.

4. ———. 2004. Loss, Trauma, and Human Resilience: Have We Underestimated the Human Capacity to Thrive Under Extremely Aversive Events? *American Psychologist* 59(1):20–28.

Chapter 10

1. Aurelius, M. 2006. *The Meditations of Marcus Aurelius.* Translated by George Long. London: Sacred Wisdom.

2. Kubzansky, L. D., and I. Kawachi. 2000. Going to the Heart of the Matter: Do Negative Emotions Cause Coronary Heart Disease? *Journal of Psychosomatic Research* 48:323–337.

3. Fuhrman, J. 2012. *Eat to Live,* Revised Edition. New York: Little Brown and Company.

4. http://www.catholic.org/prayers/prayer.php?p=134.

5. Robin, Diana (Ed). 1997. *Collected Letters of a Renaissance Feminist (The Other Voice in Early Modern Europe).* University of Chicago Press.

6. http://plato.stanford.edu/entries/vico/.

Chapter 11

1. Loren, S. 1984. *Women & Beauty.* New York: William Morrow and Company, Inc.

2. Ekman, P., and R. J. Davidson. 1993. Voluntary Smiling Changes Regional Brain Activity. *Psychological Science* 4(5):342–345.

3. http://en.wikipedia.org/wiki/Facial_feedback_hypothesis.

4. Keltner, D., and G. Bonanno. 1997. A Study of Laughter and Dissociation: Distinct Correlates of Laughter and Smiling During Bereavement. *Journal of Personality and Social Psychology* 73(4):687–702.

5. Ibid.

Chapter 12

1. Loren, S. 1984. *Women & Beauty.* New York: William Morrow and Company, Inc., p. 195.

2. Ball, D. 2006. Women in Italy Like to Clean but Shun the Quick and Easy. http://online.wsj.com/article/SB114593112611534922-search.html?

3. WNHU. 2012. In an interview with Raeleen Mautner on the Art of Living Well. November 12.

4. Ball, D. 2006. Women in Italy Like to Clean but Shun the Quick and Easy. http://online.wsj.com/article/SB114593112611534922-search.html?

Chapter 13

1. Castiglione, B. Translated by L. E. Opdyke. 1903. *The Book of the Courtier.* New York: Charles Scribner's Sons, p. 36. http://archive.org/stream/bookofcourtier00castuoft#page/n11/mode/2up.

2. Bargh, J. A., and M. J. Ferguson. 2000. Beyond Behaviorism: On the Automaticity of Higher Mental Processes. *Psychological Bulletin* 126(6):925–945.

3. Charness, N., E. Reingold, M. Pomplun, and D. Stampe. 2001. The Perceptual Aspect of Skilled Performance in Chess: Evidence from Eye Movements. *Memory & Cognition* 29(8):1146–1152.

4. Klopsch, L. 2005. *Many Thoughts of Many Minds: A Treasury of Quotations from the Literature of Every Land and Every Age.* http://www.gutenberg.org/dirs/1/7/1/1/17112/17112.txt.

Chapter 14

1. Freud, S. 2012. *The Origin and Development of Psychoanalysis.* UK: Acheron Press.

2. Maslow, A. H. 1954. *Motivation and Personality.* New York: Harper & Brothers.

3. Aurelius, M. 2006. *The Meditations of Marcus Aurelius.* Translated by George Long. London: Sacred Wisdom, p.42.

Chapter 15

1. Cicero, M. T. 1971. *Cicero: Selected Works.* London: Penguin Books, p. 86.

2. http://allpoetry.com/poem/8527623-The_Lonely_Sparrow-by-Count_Giacomo_Leopardi. English version of Leopardi's "Lonely Sparrow."

3. Rogers, C. 1980. *A Way of Being.* New York: Mariner Books.

4. Maslow, A. H. 1954. *Motivation and Personality.* New York: Harper & Brothers.

Chapter 16

1. Barducci, M. 2012. Personal communication. September 11, 2012.

2. Tumori: 65% causato da cibo e fumo (12-3-2011). http://www.primadanoi.it/news/salute/4786/Tumori-65—causato-da-cibo-e-fumo—campagna-prevenzione-Lilt.html.

3. Keys, A. 1980. *Seven Countries: A Multivariate Analysis of Death and Coronary Heart Disease.* Boston: Harvard University Press.

4. Mautner, R. D., S. V. Owen, and A. Furnham. 2000. Cross-Cultural Explanations of Body Image Disturbance in Western Cultural Samples. *International Journal of Eating Disorders* 28(2):165–172.

5. Gli uomini preferiscono le "morbide," le magre meno seduttive. http://wwwext.ansa.it/saluteebenessere/notizie/rubriche/stilidivita/2012/05/24/uomini-preferiscono-morbide-magre-meno-seduttive_6927171.html.

6. Dieta mediterranea salva la memoria. http://www.ansa.it/saluteebenessere/collection/rubriche/alimentazione/2012/03/17/visualizza_new.html_133691738.html.

Chapter 17

1. Diamanti, I. 2009. Stressati e felici, gli italiani e la crisi. July 16. Larepubblica.it http://www.repubblica.it/2009/01/sezioni/politica/mappe/mappe-16-luglio/mappe-16-luglio.html?ref=search.

2. Bandura, A. 1985. *Social Foundations of Thought and Action: A Social Cognitive Theory.* New York: Pearson.

Chapter 18

1. Choi, C. Q. 2007. Sense of Beauty Partly Innate, Study Suggests. *Live Science*, Nov. 21. http://www.livescience.com/7389-sense-beauty-partly-innate-study-suggests.html.

2. Ferrucci, P. 2009. *Beauty and the Soul: The Extraordinary Power of Everyday Beauty to Heal Your Life.* New York: Penguin.

3. Ibid.

4. Campbell, D. 2001. *The Mozart Effect: Tapping the Power of Music to Heal the Body, Strengthen the Mind, and Unlock the Creative Spirit.* Maryland: Quill (reprint edition), p. xiv.

5. Ferrucci, P. 2009. *Beauty and the Soul: The Extraordinary Power of Everyday Beauty to Heal Your Life.* New York: Penguin.

6. Loren, S. 1984. *Women & Beauty.* New York: William Morrow and Company, Inc.

7. Ferrara, J. 2012. Personal communication. May 4, 2012.

8. Konlaan, B. B. 2012. Visiting the Cinema, Concerts, Museums or Art Exhibitions as Determinant of Survival: A Swedish Fourteen-Year Cohort Follow-Up. *Scandinavian Journal of Public Health* 28(3):174–178.

9. Designer bicycles in Italy http://donna.fanpage.it/se-la-bici-diventa-fashion-stili-e-accessori-per-pedalate-eco-sostenibili/.

Chapter 19

1. Belloni, A. 2012. Personal communication. April 18, 2012.

2. Koch, S., K. Morlinghaus, and T. Fuchs. 2007. The Joy Dance: Specific Effects of a Single Dance Intervention on Psychiatric Patients with Depression. *Arts in Psychotherapy* 34:340–349.

3. Haboush, A., M. Floyd, J. Caron, M. LaSota, and K. Alvarez. 2006. Ballroom Dance Lessons for Geriatric Depression: An Exploratory Study. *Arts in Psychotherapy* 33:89–97.

4. World Health Organization. 2012. Depression. http://www.who.int/mental_health/manage ment/depression/definition/en/.

5. Koch, S., K. Morlinghaus, and T. Fuchs. 2007. The Joy Dance: Specific Effects of a Single Dance Intervention on Psychiatric Patients with Depression. *Arts in Psychotherapy* 34:340–349.

6. Ianzito, C. 2011. The Healing Powers of Dance. *AARP: The Magazine,* March 24.

7. http://www.adta.org/Default.aspx?pageId=406847. Marian Chace, American Dance Therapy Association.

8. Haboush, A., M. Floyd, J. Caron, M. LaSota, and K. Alvarez. 2006. Ballroom Dance Lessons for Geriatric Depression: An Exploratory Study. *Arts in Psychotherapy* 33:89–97.

Chapter 30

1. Gelb, M. 2000. *How to Think Like Michelangelo: Seven Steps to Genius Every Day.* New York: Dell.

2. Ferrucci, P. 2009. *Beauty and the Soul: The Extraordinary Power of Everyday Beauty to Heal Your Life.* New York: Penguin, p. 99.

3. Johnson, P. 2002. *The Renaissance: A Short History.* New York: Modern Library.

4. Mautner, R. D. 2002. *Living la Dolce Vita: Bring the Passion, Laughter, and Serenity of Italy into Your Daily Life.* IL: Sourcebooks, Inc.

Epilogue

1. Seneca: On Festivals and Fasting. Letter XVIII. http://thriceholy.net/Texts/Letter18.html.

About the Author

Raeleen D'Agostino Mautner, PhD, is a self-help specialist who advocates preserving Italian cultural wisdom and traditions as the road to physical and emotional well-being. She is an internationally acclaimed author, speaker, and radio personality. Dr. Mautner is the producer and host of "The Art of Living Well" weekly radio show on WNHU 88.7FM (www.newhaven.edu/wnhu), called "The show that can change your life" by the *New Haven Register*. She served as a behavioral expert and media and PR strategist for several studies at Yale University and also taught stress reduction strategies for a cardiac study at Yale.

A dual citizen of the United States and Italy, Dr. Mautner holds a PhD in educational/cognitive psychology and an MA in general/clinical psychology. In addition to an Italian cultural approach to self-help, she also specializes in psychology self-help techniques rooted in research. Her doctoral dissertation involved a U.S.–Italy comparison on body image disturbance. She is a former psychology professor and author of *Living la Dolce Vita: Bring the Passion, Laughter, and Serenity of Italy into Your Daily Life* (Sourcebooks, Inc), which has been translated into several languages. Dr. Mautner has also written articles for *Psychology Today,* the *Chicago Tribune,* eDiets.com, *Quirk's Marketing Research, Fra Noi, Italian America, America Oggi,* and *The Italian Tribune.* Her work has been cited in Seventeen.com, *Family Circle, First for Women, Mind/Body/Spirit, Elle,* and Weightwatchers.ca. She has appeared on national radio and television and has given presentations in the United States and Italy. To find out more, visit her blog at http://raeleenmautner.com.

Index